I HAVE SEEN TOO MUCH

I HAVE SEEN TOO MUCH

My Journey Toward Faith
Through Miracles

Terry Capehart
and a Great Cloud of Witnesses

XULON PRESS

Xulon Press
2301 Lucien Way #415
Maitland, FL 32751
407.339.4217
www.xulonpress.com

Paperback ISBN-13: 978-1-6628-5387-6
Ebook ISBN-13: 978-1-6628-5388-3

ENDORSEMENTS

"Terry Capehart has shared first-hand accounts of ordinary people experiencing extraordinary miracles. Time after time, God demonstrates His power and love for us as our loving Father touches hearts and touches lives. This book chronicles over and over how the power of prayer touches the heart of the Father and how, through prayer, God has an opportunity to show Himself strong and demonstrate His love for us. This book will increase your faith and open your eyes to God's ever-present miracles".

For the kids,

Andrew Seigrist

Dr. Andrew Seigrist
Superintendent
Tidehaven ISD

"Terry is brilliant in his depiction of miracles in his life as well as the lives of others he has known. His account of the divine encounters with people in need of prayer brings the unsuspecting reader along on the journey of racking points up for heaven and making the devil mad! It is evident that this book was a calling on his life in spite of his most recent health challenges. It is a testament that no matter what you are going through, God being for you is more than the world against you."

Rona Stringfellow
City Administrator
City of Wilmer

"Terry captures real life examples of the miracles that still happen today. A great illustration of God still at work!"

Lawrence Crow
Business Development Manager
Bureau Veritas
Plano, Texas

Table of Contents

BEGINNINGS

L ooking back for at least fifty years and being either a direct eyewitness or a longtime acquaintance of the eyewitnesses to such supernatural events that can only be described as miracles, where do I begin? I never kept a diary with day-to-day musings; however, I had recorded many of these events in the margins of my Bible or in a prayer journal, often without dates. How was I to know that one day the Holy Spirit would put it in my heart to write down all the miracles I was so blessed to witness? So, I guess I should start with the incident that served as the driving force behind the impulse to record the myriad of miracles and answered prayers that I have experienced over my lifetime. Just like you, I, too, have many questions. In sharing what I have seen and heard; it is my hope that I can provide some answers to you. The chief of these is, why do miracles still occur? Why don't more miracles occur? How come they happen to some people and not someone else, presumably more deserving?

These answers always seemed to elude me until I searched the scriptures, and there in plain sight were the answers. Unfortunately, I waited until I was a senior citizen before I discovered the answers. Hopefully, by the end of this book I will have answered your questions to your satisfaction. I feel God must have restrained me from writing about these miracles until I was ready to give Him the full honor and glory He deserves. It is with full awareness that I can only give God the credit for miracles. It is not by faith alone or willingness to pray that precipitates miracles but only when we dwindle into nothingness and weakness does God show His great power, grace, and mercy. So, read on.

Come and hear, all who fear God,
And I will tell of what He has done for my soul. (Ps. 66:16)

It started with Christmas this year. On Christmas Eve every year, we have our extended families and kids over for a large celebration and an evening of fun and gift giving. I have a hard time keeping up with just how many grandchildren and great-grandchildren we have altogether. I told my wife Linda, I needed help counting how many grandchildren and great-grandchildren we have, to which she replied with a laugh, "Good luck with that"!

I had been telling everyone we had eighteen grandkids and eight great-grandkids until Easter several years ago. I had them all sit on our steps at the lake house for a picture and discovered I had miscounted. I took out our recent Christmas list, and the actual count now officially stands at seventeen grandkids and sixteen great-grandkids! As this goes to press, we have another two great-grandchildren on the way. So, as you can imagine, we had quite a crowd. It reminded me that they are not cheaper by the dozen! I tease Linda that if someone steals her credit card, I would just let them have it because they would spend less than she did for Christmas.

On the other hand, Christmas Day is quite different in that all the families with kids stay home to wait for Santa, and the empty nesters come over for a big dinner. I had prepared a couple of spiral-cut hams for the smoker on Christmas Eve, but when I got up early the next morning, I felt rather dizzy. I sat down on the couch for a while in the dark. As dawn approached, I went ahead and took the hams out to the smoker. I felt very dizzy and was unsteady walking around the yard. I was pretty sure by this time I was having a stroke. My symptoms included double vision and a curious numbness in my hands. I never had any of the typical symptoms associated with a stroke, such as paralysis or speech problems just the double vision and a little trouble walking. I didn't panic or have a sense of urgency because the symptoms were fairly mild. I just wanted everyone coming over for dinner to have a good time and continued smoking the hams until about 10 a.m. at which time I took the hams inside to finish them off in the oven. I know it was really stupid of me to delay calling 911, but I just wanted to get things done before I went to the hospital. As soon as I got inside, I told Linda to call an ambulance because I was sure I was having a stroke.

The ambulance arrived and transported me to the hospital in Rockwall, and then I was transferred to downtown Dallas. When I finally arrived at my room at Presbyterian Hospital, I could sense a dark presence in the room. It wasn't fear, anxiety, or anything like that, but it felt more like someone or something was watching me. I could feel righteous anger rise up inside me and knew exactly what it was. I thought of one of the names of Satan, Beelzebub, so I said a quick prayer, "Bub, you don't belong in here; there is nothing you can do to shake my faith. *I have seen too much*, so get out of here, Bub, in the name of Jesus, Amen!"

The answer to my prayer was immediate, and it was as if the sun had suddenly appeared from behind the clouds. I never felt the same dark presence again. Later, that afternoon, the on-duty doctor came in to check on me and asked me the usual routine mental health questions like, "Are you feeling depressed or have you considered harming yourself or are you fearful?" I almost felt offended by this line of questioning, and I emphatically replied, "Of course not, I have no worries at all, I know what is going on because I have been through this all before." (I had made a complete recovery from a previous stroke on November 5, 2019) The doctor replied, "You have a surprisingly positive attitude, considering what just happened to you. Keep it up."

It wasn't until I got home from the hospital that I began thinking about that prayer, and I realized I really have seen too much! Thus, the inspiration for the title for this book. I can't claim to have any more faith than the next Christian by any means, and I certainly can't explain why I have been blessed so incredibly over the years. In the words of John Newton in his immortal hymn, "Amazing Grace," *"Amazing Grace how sweet the sound, that saved a wretch like me! I once was lost, but now am found; was blind, **but now I see**,"* and boy, have I seen things! I have witnessed first-hand and received news of miracles, healings, divine appointments, fulfilled prophecies, and answered prayers just to name a few.

In the following chapters, I will describe all these types of miracles, from the common everyday miracles we take for granted, such as, the beauty of nature, our families, and just being alive to the 'sure 'nuff' miracles that are of biblical proportions that defy our understanding of how our universe is 'supposed' to work. I even delve into the difficult issues, such as, why sometimes the miracles we so desperately need and want just don't happen. I am willing to tread on the thin ice of cultural hot buttons by taking on the subject of 'truth' and abortion. Finally, I present a number of useful tools to use in everyday life to share the gospel with others, fight spiritual battles and build up our families. Enjoy the journey along with me of how my faith has been made unshakeable by experiencing one miracle after another.

SILENT WITNESS

I first started experiencing unbelievably powerful and wonderful encounters with the Holy Spirit and answers to my prayers as far back as when I attended Stephen F. Austin State University in Nacogdoches in East Texas in the mid-seventies. Looking back, I can see how many times my prayers, and the prayers of my prayer partners, were answered in dramatic fashion. Seeing such strong answers to prayer, I developed such a strong confidence within me that my prayer life became exciting and invigorating. I soon began to have a boldness that I knew hadn't been there before. Over the years, I began to take the lead for the family prayers at Thanksgiving and other gatherings. It soon became expected that I would lead the group in prayer. The consequences of praying at family gatherings really came home to me when my grandkids started asking me to baptize them.

In fact, as I am writing this, I am taking an online ordination class to become a credentialed wedding officiant in order to officiate at my grandson, Jacob's, wedding in May of 2022. Jacob told his mother, Tricia, that he wanted to just get married by a Justice of the Peace, and his mom told him, "Okay let's just have the wedding in our backyard." Jacob told his mother, "I would like Terry to perform the ceremony then." Tricia called me just shortly after my seventieth birthday to see if I would officiate at Jacob's wedding, and of course I agreed. I am claiming this as one of the best birthday gifts I have ever received. By the way, it is now June and the wedding went off without a hitch Well, I guess there was <u>ONE</u> hitch, ha!

Our faith hasn't been something that we flaunt, heaven forbid! We are all repulsed by someone with a self-righteous, holier-than-thou attitude. Our steadfast faith has come about in much more subtle ways as when the family is over at our house. Our Bibles are always on the little stand next to the couch in the living room where we try to read from our Bibles as often as we can. They see us practice our faith in so many ways that we are not even aware we're doing it anymore. But they take notice and every once in a while, they mention it to someone else in the family, and it eventually finds its way back home. I have to admit that it gives me great satisfaction when a grandchild or great-grandchild notices that we say grace at mealtimes and ask if they can pray too. Besides that, it just warms our hearts again and again.

After my first stroke, my wife and I decided it was about time to draw up our wills and create the necessary powers of attorney. We asked Linda's daughter, Shelly, and my youngest daughter, Anna, to be the executors of our estate. Anna surprised us when she replied, "The only thing I really want from your estate is your well-worn, marked-up Bible!" It could not have meant more to me as a father than that! Anna's request to have my well-worn Bible thrilled my heart and soul. I also have the well-worn Bibles of my mom and dad (Lorraine and Donald Sam Capehart). So, it has worked out perfectly that my oldest daughter, Chari, will get my mom's Bible and my son, Sam, will get my father's Bible, whom he is named after. It is a tremendous comfort to me and confidence builder when our children validate their faith in us like that. I don't always feel all that faithful from day to day, but when one of our kids say they are inspired by watching us, peace that passes all understanding just pushes out the worries of the day.

Andrew shared with me, "After my father died, Mom called us to the house after the funeral to divide Dad's belongings. My brother-in -law and brother chose tools from Dad's shop and garage. We were all out there in the shop, my mom, brother and his wife, brother-in-law and my sister, my wife Angela and me. My brother and brother-in-law were going from tool to tool and deciding who would get what. I chose a few small things for myself but mostly stood way back (I had a plan for what I wanted.) The tools were 'things' Dad worked with. What I truly wanted was Dad's Bible study materials, his books, and notes. *Those* had my dad's fingerprints and his mind of Christ in every page.

"Finally, my brother could see that I was laying back, and he stopped and said, "You haven't claimed hardly anything. What do you want from Dad?" I smiled and replied, "I want his Bible study books and his notes." My brother instantly saw the wisdom in it and he said, "They are yours," with a grin. He said, "I work mostly with my hands. You work mostly with your mind. You will get more use out of Dad's books than me or Jeff.

"Then I suddenly realized that my Dad's greatest notes and thoughts of Christ were already written within me, within my heart, and that my father himself taught them every single day. My father did not withhold any wisdom from me to give to me upon his death. My dad poured in the wisdom of God every single day of my life. *That* is why I have deep roots, and *that* is why I am strong in the Lord and the power of His might. I stand upon the sacrifices and teachings of my earthly father, Earl Seigrist. My hero and model for my own family."

Life always seems to throw you curve balls to see if you are alert. If you are paying close attention, you will notice the more you draw closer to God the more the enemy tries to strike you out. I have had my share of ups and downs like anyone else. It is a fact of life; if you are still breathing, you will be guaranteed to have 'those' days in which it is just hard to feel the presence of the Holy Spirit. I just have to ask myself, "If I don't feel very close to God, then who moved?" The events I am sharing with you here are a great reminder that Jesus is always right by our side no matter what may be happening around us. For this reason, a number of years ago, I chose the following *Psalm 139:23–24* to be my life verses to remind me to stay the course every day:

Search me, O God, and know my heart; Try me and know my anxious thoughts; and see if there be any hurtful way in me, and lead me in the everlasting way. **(Ps. 139: 23–24)**

We are constantly under the watchful eyes of our family, friends, co-workers, and strangers, but it is especially true of our children. I am reminded of the time I was living in Seattle back in the early eighties. My son Sam was four years old at the time. He was playing in the backyard while I was working on the car in the garage. I stuck my head out from under the hood and cleared my throat and spit on the grass. From across the yard, I heard him clear his throat and spit in a perfect imitation of me. It was then I realized that he was watching my every move and everything I said or did even from a distance. The Holy Spirit really convicted me that day that I should be more engaged as a father and more cognizant of the Christian witness I was projecting.

We made the decision then and there to get our kids in church as soon as possible. We started attending St. Elizabeth's Episcopal Church in Burien, Washington. From the somewhat stodgy reputation Episcopal liturgical services have, you would never have guessed that some of the most incredible miracles would come from within their doors. That old truism, "You can't judge a book by its cover" was certainly true here.

Children are like sponges, like the old adage states. They soak up everything around them, so it also very wise to monitor their friends, television programming, and social media early on. You are not, I repeat *not*, invading their privacy to see what they are doing on social media, watching on television, or what they are doing with their friends. So many people have regretted not intervening sooner into their child's life before they suffered a fatal drug overdose or committed suicide. We are stewards of the lives God places in our hands; let's not allow the enemy take our children and loved ones from us. Fight back with all your might.

In closing this chapter, remember we carry the awesome responsibility, as Christians, of projecting the spotless and holy character of Jesus to everyone around us. Not that we are perfect by any stretch of the imagination, but rather always being mindful of the fact that our behavior is often the only experience many will have of the love of Christ. Your 'silent witness' is far more powerful than you realize.

DIVINE APPOINTMENTS

Over the years, my confidence in prayers has greatly increased as I have seen so many prayers answered in a spectacular way. Prayer has now become second nature to me, and I have found that the Holy Spirit often prompts me to pray for people, even total strangers. These 'divine' appointments just happen spontaneously but are unmistakably the work of the Holy Spirit. We have to learn to carry a prayer around in our hearts, and when the opportunity arises, you just take it out and share it.

I came out of retirement in 2018, working as the Municipal Development Director for the City of Lancaster south of Dallas. I went to lunch at a Luby's Cafeteria, and as I was about to pay for my lunch, I thought I was prompted to say something to the cashier. He was a tall, slim young man about twenty years old, and I said, "I am about to say grace over my food. Do you have any prayer requests?" He just smiled but didn't say anything, but an elderly lady who was waiting for her take out order, turned to me and said, "My fifty-year-old son just died yesterday from a sudden heart attack, and I could sure use some prayer"! I knew then the Holy Spirit was the one prompting me to step out in faith and in prayer. People all around us are hurting desperately, and if not for the Holy Spirit, they would be invisible, unnoticed, and overlooked. My prayer partner, Andrew, and I always ask God to send people into our paths, who we can witness to or pray for.

Later that year, I was on the way home from a city council meeting, and I stopped at Lindy's Restaurant in Mesquite to grab a bite to eat. Once again, I asked the waitress if she had any prayer requests as I was getting ready to say grace. She had a very surprised look on her face as she related that her husband's grandmother had just passed away and that he was very close to her. Tears streamed down her face as I prayed with her.

As I mentioned earlier, these events can occur at any time and any place. I went to a restaurant in Arlington, Texas, to meet my daughter, Chari, and her family for supper. I was running about thirty minutes late, but according to God's watch, I was right on time. As I got out of my pickup truck to enter the restaurant, I noticed an elderly woman attempting to step over the curb. Suddenly she tripped, losing her balance, and as she fell, I grabbed her arm to lift her back up right. She apologized and explained that she had just undergone some major heart surgery and was still weak. As we went up the wheelchair ramp together, I asked her if I could pray for her. Both she and I received a blessing that day. I am reminded of the Bible verse that says, "It is more blessed to give than to receive." If you don't feel blessed when you get to pray for someone, you need to open the eyes of your heart and see the miracle directly in front of you.

An unexpected encounter happened when I was on my way to my consulting job in Wilmer, Texas, by way of the very congested freeway, Interstate 635, that encircles Dallas. In the early morning rush hour, I suddenly felt my truck lurch to the right,

and I immediately knew I had a flat tire. I managed to nego-
tiate my way through several lanes of heavy traffic and found
a relative level area of shoulder to safely pull off the roadway.
I retrieved the jack from the truck and was in the process of
taking off the lug nuts when a good Samaritan pulled over in
front of me and got out and asked if I needed some help. I
replied, "I think I just about got it." The man hollered, "Okay,"
and got back in his car and drove off. So, I went back to the task
at hand, and I soon discovered the wheel was rusted so badly it
was frozen on the hub and wouldn't budge. I called a tire shop
nearby and was informed no tire shop would conduct roadside
assistance on IH 635 because of the risk of working in heavy
traffic. They suggested that I call a wrecker and have it towed to
the tire shop. With visions of having to spend over a hundred
dollars to fix a flat, I said a quick prayer, "Lord, I am sorry I sent
away your first guardian angel; could you send me another one,
please"? I was standing next to the truck with the passenger
door open and before I could even put my phone down on the
seat, another car pulled in behind me. God had sent another
guardian angel to help me. The man knew just how to get the
tire off. With a can of spray lubricant and a swift kick, the tire
popped loose. When he finished, he even loaded the flat tire in
the back of my truck. Wow, I don't think I ever enjoyed a flat
tire so much!

I am reminded of the anecdote of an elderly couple who had
just passed away. Standing together, they were led into a large
room that had floor to ceiling file cabinets. When they asked the
accompanying angel, "What do all the files contain"? The angel
replied, "These files all contain information about you!" The
couple incredulously answered, "How can that be"? The angel
replied, "These are all the things God wanted you to have but

you didn't ask for"! Do you think you have prayed about everything you should have? *Think again!*

One of the first and most powerful divine appointments I ever had with the Holy Spirit occurred in 1976 while enrolled at Stephen F. Austin State University (SFA). I attended SFA on the GI Bill after I was discharged from the Navy in November 1974. I think it was probably the pivotal event that launched this incredible journey of my 'eyes-wide-open' faith. I could state, "my cup runneth over," but that would be a tremendous understatement, more like a fifty-gallon barrel!

I enrolled at SFA in the summer of 1975 and applied for a job as a janitor at the student center. My primary duty was to set up banquet rooms for various events. One particular evening in the fall of 1976, Titus Stein and I went to get a room ready for the women from the kitchen so they could set up the tables for a banquet. Titus was a slim, dapper-looking man in his early fifties with a small mustache reminiscent of Errol Flynn. As partners we would always work these events together. We had a habit of returning right at the end of the banquet because the kitchen staff always saved us pieces of pie or cake, sort of perks of the job you might say.

On this particular night, when we showed up at the room, a female student was helping the regular kitchen staff who were all older women. She and I were the only ones who sat down at the table while everyone else remained standing, including Titus who stood silently by the door. The young lady and I started to have a casual conversation that somehow turned to a discussion about Eastern meditation and religion. All of a sudden, I began to give incredibly powerful rebuttals to everything she said she believed in. I was able to share my faith that countered every point in her belief system. It wasn't condescending or insulting, but just the powerful truth of the Holy Spirit on full display. We never raised our voices, if anything it was the calm manner in which I spoke that gave the impression of the absolute authority in what I was saying. No one else ever said a word, and you could feel the palpable power in the room. When it was over, we just ate our dessert as usual and finished cleaning the room in silence. I went home that night, confident I gave the devil a black eye.

The next day as I was cutting through the kitchen to get on the service elevator, and one of the women in the kitchen who had not been there the night before confronted me and jokingly waved her finger in my face, scolding me that if I was to ever preach again that I had better invite the rest of the kitchen staff. So powerful was the manifestation of the Holy Spirit the night before, that word spread I was a preacher. The odd thing was that I never had another opportunity to share my faith with that student and I never saw the other student again. I don't remember a word of what I said. I found out later that the message I gave that night wasn't meant entirely for that student at all although it might have been.

Whenever I share the gospel, I have always wondered, "Does the seed ever come to harvest?" I am sure I have gotten to harvest the seed planted by others but up to that point I had never seen anyone ever commit themselves to the Lord that I had witnessed to. I have always imagined the 'treasure' we have waiting for us in heaven is actually those we have led to Christ.

In this case, Jesus demonstrated His most loving grace to me in that I got to see the harvest. As I sit typing this manuscript, forty-five years later, the tears are so thick in my eyes right now I can barely see to type. You see, that student wasn't the object of my witnessing but rather Titus was. Titus died from cancer the day before Thanksgiving, just two months later. At his funeral, our supervisor, Johnny, took me aside and told me not worry about where Titus was going. He said that the night of the banquet Titus was so moved by the demonstration of the power of the Holy Spirit that the following Sunday he went to church with his family and gave his life to Christ and was subsequently baptized. Titus never told me this, and Johnny said that Titus would bring a small pocket New Testament to work and when things were slow, he would go hide in a closet or empty room and read his Bible. I can't help but believe that Titus will be one of my neighbors in heaven. Amen!

I have learned we are sowing seeds of truth even if we are not aware of it. Just like my son imitating me from a distance, which at the time I was totally unaware of, God puts people in our path every single day. Just as the warning that, "we may be entertaining angels unawares," we need to open our eyes to those around us with a new perspective, a new focus that we have been sent to witness on purpose. What we think are accidental encounters are intentionally orchestrated by God! Wow, now that is a thought!

WHAT IS TRUTH?

I want to pause for a moment and discuss something that is near and dear to my heart, and that is the subject of truth, especially in the context of the 'cancel' and 'woke' cultures today. With the standard narrative in the so-called 'news' media, social media, politicians, and the like, we have finally reached the point that the truth is now considered to be a lie and lies are now considered to be the truth. Without the discernment of the Holy Spirit, how can Christians anywhere discern what is truth?

> *and all the ways that wickedness deceives those who are perishing. They perish because they refused to love the truth and so be saved. For this reason, God sends them a powerful delusion so that they will believe the lie. (2 Thess. 2:10–11)*

It is a sad reality that the talk of miracles and the movement of the Holy Spirit cannot be openly expressed in an arena of public debate without the risk of a blistering attack on our character and possibly our careers. I don't think any discussion of basic Christian fundamentals and core beliefs can be made without the understanding of what truth is and is not. This is where I feel

I must address the issue of *truth*, as in the now-famous dialogue in the movie, *A Few Good Men (Columbia Pictures, 1992)*:

JESSEP: You want answers?
KAFFEE: I want the truth!
JESSEP: You can't handle the truth!

I know there is the usual cadre of those who consider themselves woke. They are actually more accurately described as doubters, scoffers, haters, progressives, atheists, materialists, and others of the politically correct crowd. These individuals are totally void of faith, just waiting for the chance to mock and criticize anything even hinting at manifestations of the supernatural much less of the Christian faith. I want say a word to them directly, as an eyewitness to supernatural miracles, I could care less what their objections are as they have absolutely no bearing on the truth.

For the word of the cross is foolishness to those who are perishing, but to us who are being saved it is the power of God.
(1 Cor. 1:18)

So, according to scripture, these unbelievers are defined as being, *foolish*! I won't waste my time casting pearls before swine *(Matt. 7:6)*. If you find yourself in this category, then I suggest you put this book down as quickly as possible before the 'Truth' begins to set you free! Now I ask you: "If God, Jesus, and Christianity were true, would you be willing to believe?" If the answer is yes, then you are simply ignorant of the truth and have a 'head issue'. If you are still not willing to believe, then you have a 'heart issue'.

Speaking of truth: truth doesn't require anyone to believe in it to be true—it simply is. Truth is, by its very nature, transcendent and immutable. Truth is not changed by time, circumstances, history, culture, or anything external to itself. Truth exists independently of man; each person does not have the license to invent his own truth. You hear it commonly said today, "This is my truth." No, that is your experience and perspective. That does not necessarily make it *the Truth*. Truth does not have anything to fear from lies, distortions, deceptions, or attacks from any source. It always remains the same, day in and day out, unaffected by the feeble imaginations of men.

Lies, on the other hand, must be believed to have any relevance. Lies can only exist in the absence of truth. Lies always live in fear of the truth; therefore, lies will always attempt to silence, weaken, destroy, attack, or corrupt the truth by any means possible. Since lies cannot coexist with the truth, lies seek to remove anyone or anything which represents or speaks the truth. When truth enters a room, the lies will always attack the truth even if they don't know why because the spirit in them senses danger to their very existence. Just try sharing true statements on social media and see what happens.

How tragically sad it must be to spend one's entire life in the vain and senseless pursuit of a Godless worldview whose sole purpose is to transmit as much misery to the rest of humankind as possible. I can only imagine how hopeless and cynical they must feel all of the time, which compels me to pray for all of those who have committed their lives to hatred, rebellion, and violence against the only hope this poor planet has—Jesus. The truth is there is only one race of people on earth, the human race all created in the image of God. It is an artificial construct to group people into classes or groups. All constitutional rights accrue to the individual not groups. In the eyes of God there are no gender rights, no minority rights, no majority rights, no racial rights, no sexual orientation rights we are <u>ALL</u> children of God. Phony social constructs, which do nothing but cause hatred and anger, will become totally irrelevant when we start acting like children of God. More importantly, salvation is an individual choice. No 'group' of people are guaranteed passage to Heaven not even the 'chosen' people. My prayer is that you would come to know the Truth and the Truth will set you free.

> *So, Jesus was saying to those Jews who had believed Him, "If you continue in My word, then you are truly disciples of Mine; and you will know the truth, and the truth will make you free."* **(John 8:31–32)**

As I said in the beginning, I am an eyewitness to these events. I do not have so-called 'blind faith,' I now have 'eyes-wide-open' faith. I think it is more than appropriate that we call what we do as 'practicing' our faith. The more practice we get in on our knees, the stronger our faith becomes.

In the classic atheist's paradox (I am not sure where I heard this, but I think it bears repeating): "That they conveniently exclude themselves from hell which they claim they don't believe in and then are offended when the Bible informs them that they are excluded from heaven which also they claim not to believe in." And we know the source of lies *(John 8:44)*.

SEEING IS BELIEVING

My faith is not faith born of what the writer in Hebrews describes but is much deeper than that. Like the old adage, "Seeing is believing." Trust in Jesus is not something you can see, however, and trusting Jesus is a culmination of both the experience of having God's promises fulfilled over and over in our lives, as well as trusting Him to fulfill His promises in the future, especially the promise of our salvation.

> *Now faith is the assurance of things hoped for, the conviction of things not seen. (**Heb. 11:1**)*

> *For we did not follow cleverly devised tales when we made known to you the power and coming of our Lord Jesus Christ, but we were **eyewitnesses** of His majesty. (**2 Pet. 1:16**)*

> *And we are **witnesses** of these things; and so is the Holy Spirit, whom God has given to those who obey Him. (**Acts 5:32**)*

So why am I telling you about all the miracles I have witnessed, and why are miracles still happening today? I think everyone agrees that miracles performed by Jesus and the early church were 'signs and wonders' designed to establish the fact that they had authority directly bestowed on them by God. What are we to do when we witness or experience a life changing miracle?

I suffered a near-death experience on March 5, 2005, by nearly drowning. At first, I just could not understand why God had spared my life. Months passed, and I still didn't have any satisfactory answers. Then I was reading my Bible one day, and the words and my answer just jumped off the page. The small, still voice of the Holy Spirit could not have been more succinct and unequivocal. The answer came from the Psalms:

> *O God, You have taught me from my youth,*
> ***And I still declare Your wondrous deeds.***
> *And even when I am old and gray, O God, do not forsake me,*
> ***Until I declare Your strength to this generation. (Ps. 71:17–18)***

The answer seems obvious now. Whenever we are witnesses to a miracle or any other manifestation of God's power, blessings, answered prayer, or the work of the Holy Spirit, we have a duty—no, an obligation—to tell others as the Psalmist declares. Since that fateful day, I have found over and over when I witness to someone by quoting scriptures in the traditional method of sharing the Gospel, it is not nearly as effective as telling someone what Jesus has done for me personally. At least it is easier to open the conversation with a miracle I had witnessed before quoting the scriptures.

It is still hard for me to understand why I have witnessed so many miracles. I certainly can't say that I deserve them, and then no one could possibly make that claim. However, I have come to expect miracles to happen. My eyes are now open to the possibility of witnessing a miracle, and so I am continually watching for miracles to occur. I don't intend to say I have a special gift or any claim to corner the market on miracles. But I do believe God is so faithful and so full of love and grace that I do expect God to answer prayers and perform miracles.

When it does happen, I feel like falling on my knees in humble adoration and thanksgiving. The lyrics of Cory Asbury's song, "Reckless Love," "I couldn't earn it, and I don't deserve it, still You give Yourself away," says it all. No matter how many times my prayers are not answered in the way I want them to, I will never hesitate to ask God for another miracle. Someone once defined a problem as the difference between what you expect to get and what you actually get. I have never ever had a problem whatsoever with God. What I mean by expecting another miracle is that I believe it is in the very nature of God to answer our prayers and perform miracles; it is what He does! I don't expect Him to perform at my demand or command like some of the prosperity doctrines claim. I just expect Him to do what He has always done and continues to do. In that, I have complete faith and trust. It is a real comfort to me to know that God can perform a real miracle anytime He so wills.

> *What was from the beginning, what we have heard, what we have **seen with our eyes**, what we have looked at and touched with our hands, concerning the Word of Life and the life was revealed, and **we have seen and testify** and proclaim to you the eternal life, which was with the Father and was revealed to us what we have seen and heard we proclaim to you also, so that you too may have fellowship with us; and indeed our fellowship is with the Father, and with His Son Jesus Christ. **These things we write**, so that our joy may be made complete. (**John 1:4**)*

SURE-'NUFF MIRACLES

I n today's cynical world, do miracles of biblical proportions still occur? Tim Wildmon hosts a show called, "Miracle Monday," on American Family Radio, in which he talks about 'Sure 'Nuff' miracles. Tim invited me several years ago to give my testimony of several of the miracles mentioned in this book on the radio. To the question of "'Do miracles happen today?" I emphatically say, "Yes." I have seen miracles with my own eyes!

In December of 1978, we moved to Seattle, Washington, so I could go to graduate school at the University of Washington to get my master's degree in Forest Genetics. I needed just one class to finish up my bachelor's degree in Forestry from SFA. As it turned out, it became very difficult to get started on my graduate work. One day I realized that my undergraduate classes would begin expiring after seven years, so in desperation, I contacted the SFA registrar's office and was able to get a letter accepting one advanced forestry class to complete my degree. I completed the class in 1982, and I fulfilled my bachelor's degree just in the nick of time.

About the same time all this was going on, the realization that my son was watching my every move, prompted me to have a more positive influence on my children. When we started attending St. Elizabeth's Episcopal Church, Father Jon Lindenauer was the pastor who was a former army chaplain in Vietnam and even served in a combat zone. As a Navy Vietnam veteran, myself, I found I could really relate to him, and they had wonderful youth programs as well. It didn't take long, and we felt right at home.

St. Elizabeth's had a folk music group called Hosea that led the services on Fridays with guitars, banjos, flutes, and tambourines. My wife and I soon joined the group not as musicians, but as part of the choir that could only be described as a 'joyful noise.' Clearly my best singing moments came in the shower! Every Saturday afternoon, we would practice, in which fully half of the time was spent in prayer. The banjo player, whose name escapes me, had a young daughter about six years old, and on a Monday while getting ready for school, she tripped with a pencil in her hand. It was a parent's worst nightmare. The sharp end of the pencil was driven though the left eye socket and a full three inches into her brain! You just have to cringe to think of that mental image. I'll let that soak in for a minute.

As soon as the ambulance rushed her off to the hospital, the prayer chain was initiated, and we received the call about 9 o'clock in the morning. We got word later that day that the pencil had not damaged the eyeball but had pushed the eye to the side and even missed the optical nerve. She not only had no vision loss but there was no evidence of brain damage! The pencil was successfully removed, and she was released from the hospital the next day, only having to wear an eye patch for about three weeks. A parent's worst nightmare turned into the most glorious victory over fear that can be imagined. Hallelujah!

The next event happened when Anna my youngest daughter was invited to attend a swim party at the YMCA with her older sister, Chari. Anna was about eight years old at the time, and Chari was thirteen. About seven in the evening, we got a panicked call from the mother who hosted the party, stating that there had been an accident. We were totally unprepared for what we were about to be told. Anna had been found at the bottom of the pool at the deep end completely unconscious and did not respond to CPR performed at the scene.

When we got to the hospital, we were not even allowed to see Anna right away, but instead we were ushered into a small meeting room with three doctors and two nurses where we received the devasting news there was about a 90 percent chance she would have permanent brain damage. We couldn't imagine what it meant to be brain damaged that severely. I can't explain why, but neither of us were ever even afraid. In fact, it felt more like a warm comforting blanket of calm had enveloped us. We notified our prayer partners and left it in God's hands. We finally got to go in and see her and she had tubes and wires all running all over the place and was such a weird shade of bluish gray, that at first, I thought she had died. We reluctantly went home as they would not let us stay in the ICU with her. The last vision I had of her was lying lifeless and naked on that cold table with the tubes and wires sticking out everywhere without so much as a sheet for a cover.

At nine o'clock the next morning, we received news of a miracle. They called for us to come and pick Anna up as she had completely recovered with absolutely no signs of any brain damage! We excitedly called the prayer group to give the great news and thank them for their prayers and thank God for answering our desperate prayers.

Today Anna is living near Little Rock and is enrolled in Hebrew University in Jerusalem online, studying ancient biblical languages with aspirations of becoming a translator of ancient languages. Several years ago, Anna challenged me to begin studying a number of Bible scholars and apologists, such as Chuck Missler, Frank Turek, J. Warner Wallace, Stephen Meyer, John Lennox, Eric Metaxas, Jonathan Cahn, and Michael Heiser, just to name a few. I have increased my understanding of the Bible at least a hundred-fold since then. Don't like to read? Look them up on *YouTube*. You can even download the lectures as MP3 files and load them on your digital player. Sorry, you don't have any excuses now. Listen to them during your commute to work, doing yard work or while cleaning the house. It will be a fascinating fellowship with the Lord, and time flies by. You be surprised how quickly your chores are done or you arrive at your destination.

Although Anna was baptized at an early age, she had a dramatic true conversion experience when she was about twenty-four years old. This occurred before she was married, and she had just found out her then-boyfriend was cheating on her. So, after breaking up with him, she starting hanging out with a group of coworkers at Service Merchandise in Ft. Worth. The group was rather fond of partying and playing pool. A new coworker joined the workforce named Bill Weaver, and true to form, they invited him out to party after work. He stated he didn't drink or go to night clubs because he was also a pastor at a local church. Imagine if you will for a moment, that God even arranged for her new coworker to be a pastor! Immediately, the Holy Spirit began working on Anna, and she felt so embarrassed that she had invited a preacher out to party.

In any case, Anna and her friends went out alone for an evening of 'fun' and ended up going to a psychic for a reading. They all pitched in and shelled out fifty dollars for the reading. Her friends went first and all got about a twenty-to thirty-minute reading, but when Anna's turn came, the psychic couldn't read anything. Anna got mad and accused the psychic of being a phony, and they went out and found another psychic and the same thing happened again.

On the way home alone in her car she said, "Lord, I just want a relationship with You alone." The Holy Spirit said, "You need to quit smoking because I am sending you a man who doesn't smoke." She immediately rolled down the window and threw her cigarettes away and never smoked again. True to God's word, Anna met a guy named James at church, who was studying for the ministry, and they soon became engaged.

Very strange things began to happen at her work. Some guys came out of the warehouse and were cursing loudly, and it was so painful to Anna's ears she went down to her knees clapping her hands over her ears. Next, she began discerning various spirits on people, like evil spirits of lying, stealing, and even infidelity. Her fiancé's best friend was the pastor of a small church in Benbrook, Texas, and Anna saw the spirit of infidelity on him. When she mentioned it to James, he got very mad and refused to believe it. Later that week, James just popped in unannounced at the pastor's house and found a young woman with him, and his wife was not with them. Two or three weeks later, the pastor ran off with the woman, and the church dissolved. Anna's vision of the spirit of infidelity on the pastor was correct.

She told Bill Weaver about it and said she was going to stop wearing her glasses because she couldn't stand seeing all the evil. Bill told her she had a gift and don't ever quit. She started reading her Bible, and the way she described it was like the words literally jumped off the page as if in three dimensions.

It was like tasting honey; the words were so sweet to her mind. The revelations she received while reading her Bible astounded her, and the scriptures came alive. This special dispensation lasted only a couple more months. She soon got married to James, and when her store manager offered her a job at their Little Rock store, with that opportunity in hand, they moved to Arkansas, and as they say the rest is history.

Since she now lives in Arkansas, we have to carry on long-distance conversations. Our discussions can only be described as 'iron sharpening iron' *(Prov. 27:17)*. It seems to me God wasn't finished with her yet. When she and her husband decided to move to Arkansas where he was from, I teased my son-in-law that he was about to raise the IQ of both states, her moving to Arkansas and him leaving Texas! Bwa-ha-ha-ha! I just couldn't resist.

Now back to Hosea in Seattle. We were attending a backyard church picnic at a fellow church member's house, which was situated on a beautiful private lake. While playing football with a group of men, I accidentally hit one of the men in the eye. We decided to stop playing and take a break, and every last person on the field went up to the house to get a cold drink except me. I turned to go down to the dock to look at the lake.

When I got to the end of the pier, I looked into the crystal-clear water only to see my son, Sam, sinking out of sight with a look of pure terror on his face as he was drowning. I have an image of that look permanently burned into my brain. I will always remember that look on his face. I instantly jumped into the water and pulled Sam up to the surface where he began coughing and choking. Poor Sam, it had never occurred to him that he could not swim (he was about six years old at the time). This happened just a very short time after the above incident with my daughter, Anna at the swim party at the YMCA, and I clearly heard the Holy Spirit tell me, "I have taken your children away from you, and now I have given them back to you—*Now*, what are you going to do with them?" Shortly afterward, the YMCA called to offer free swimming lessons for all my kids, which we gladly accepted.

I have already introduced you to Hosea, the folk music gospel group at St. Elizabeth's Episcopal church. One Saturday, I was asked to stand in for Marvin Butterfield at the following Monday's Christian Businessmen's breakfast meeting at the Holiday Inn near SeaTac airport. Marvin had been diagnosed with a blood clot in his neck, so we prayed for him before he went in for surgery Monday morning. Marvin had served in the Korean War and had been shot in the stomach during the war and, among other things, had one of his kidneys removed along with two of his ribs. After emergency surgery to stabilize him in Seoul, he was flown to Portland, Oregon, to have the rest of the surgery performed at the VA hospital. Also, since the Korean War, Marvin had developed hardening of the arteries and had suffered four heart attacks since the war in 1952.

As Marvin was being prepared for surgery to remove the clot, the doctor told the radiologist to take it easy on the contrast dye because he had kidney problems without mentioning exactly what they were. A few minutes later the radiologist came in and triumphantly announced Marvin's kidneys were just fine. The doctor said, "Wait a minute he only has one kidney." The radiologist then said, "Well, he has two now"! So, they ran the X-rays again, and it turned out that not only did he have another kidney but further tests revealed the scar tissue from four heart attacks was gone, the blood clot was gone from his neck, and chemically his blood was like that of an eighteen-year-old.

They went so far as to have the VA records sent from Portland, Oregon, to verify his kidney had indeed been removed in 1952. I helped Marvin write a letter to the VA and declared to them he had been healed by a miracle and no longer qualified for the disability pay that he had received since his discharge in 1952. In typical government logic (or lack thereof), they said if he insisted on claiming he was not qualified for disability pay then he needed to refund all of the payments he had received from 1952 until then. He quickly replied, "Never mind!" and he never heard any more about it. The funny thing was that he still had two ribs missing. I said, "Well if Adam . . ."

Another odd thing that happened was when Marvin gave his testimony to the full church, a lot of people never came back. Over and over, we read that God is the same yesterday, today, and tomorrow, yet many Christians don't believe in modern miracles. They put their spiritual blinders on and try to keep Jesus in a safe, well-defined little box. They sit on their hands on the pews, afraid that their safe zone will be shaken up, so they don't dare ask God to answer a really difficult prayer—as if God no longer wanted to or could no longer do a miracle. What a pity. My God is more than able and willing to perform miracles! Amen! I often pray that God will send a miracle just to shake things up a bit. We all need to pray that this country will experience a spiritual shaking like never before.

And when they had prayed, the place where they had gathered together was shaken, and they were all filled with the Holy Spirit and began to speak the word of God with boldness.
(Acts 4:31)

On March 5, 2005, I had a near-death experience that changed my perspective on my life forever. After earlier relating the stories of my children nearly drowning in Seattle back in the 1980s, it was now my turn. We were now living in a newly built custom house that backed right up to City Lake Park in Royse City, Texas, and we even had a gate in our back fence that gave us direct access to the park. The grandkids loved to go for walks and feed the ducks, and we always kept stale bread on hand just in case they came over. I don't remember why or what the argument was about, but my wife and I had quite a heated discussion. So, I loaded up my fishing gear and went to the lake to go fishing just to have some quiet time alone. I had a small, twelve-foot aluminum boat that I had actually bought when I was in Seattle. I went down to the City of Garland power plant at Lake Lavon to launch the boat on the east side of the lake.

There was not so much as a breath of air stirring, and the lake was so calm it looked like a mirror. I fished for about an hour out in the main part of the lake, and I wasn't catching anything, so I went back into a cove near the Mallard Cove railroad trestle. I took off my life jacket so I could cast easier because I was still wearing a heavy coat. I caught one pretty nice bass. It began to get late, so I decided to call it quits before it got completely dark.

I headed back out to the open lake to head north to the power plant boat ramp. As I entered the open water, my right arm was getting tired holding the tiller, so I switched over to my left hand. The lake was still as smooth as glass, and I was making good time. All of a sudden, I noticed a large wave heading toward me from some boat that passed earlier from across the lake that was no longer in sight. I have negotiated hundreds of such waves in the past as I had owned that boat for over twenty years at the time.

All you have to do is cut back on the throttle, and the nose will drop down and thump, thump, you are over the wave. Instead, because my left hand was on the throttle, I inadvertently goosed the engine, and when the bow of my boat hit the wave, the boat shot nearly straight up, tossing me instantly head first into the water. It happened so suddenly, I had no time to react, and as I was trying to orient myself and figure out what happened, I realized I had not put my life jacket back on after fishing. My boat was racing in wild, tight, counterclockwise circles because the tiller slammed as far as it would go to the left and the throttle was wide open. I tried grabbing the boat but at the speed it was going and with the bow sticking up in the air, it made it impossible to catch, and there was the real danger that the boat would run me over and cut me up with the propeller.

I paused for a moment to assess my situation again and soon realized I was in very dire straits and in a very dangerous situation. The water was freezing, and I had lost one shoe. Worst of all my cell phone was soaking wet and was totally dead. I had crazy thoughts going through my head. I said matter of factly to myself, "This is the day you are going die." I even thought maybe I should get it over with and just take a big gulp of water. In the next moment, a complete calmness came over me. I overcame the panic of the situation and calmed my thoughts. Looking around for the first time I spotted my life jacket floating about sixty or seventy feet away and beyond that was my seat cushion. I dog paddled over to my life jacket and slipped it under my chest and then proceeded to retrieve the boat cushion. I was afloat! My boat was still running in tight circles so I looked around the lake and only one boat was anywhere in sight and was almost a mile away, way beyond shouting distance. I thought, "Now what?" I was over a half mile from the nearest shore and I wondered how long I could last in the cold water. I was already so cold I could barely dog paddle.

After about twenty-five minutes in the cold water, I spotted a pontoon boat in the distance headed right toward me from the direction of the power plant. Bob Nix had been in his back-yard and noticed my boat doing wild donuts in the water. Out of curiosity, he went inside and retrieved his binoculars, and when he scanned the boat, he spotted me in the water. He immediately jumped into action with no thought of calling 911. He handed the binoculars off to his wife and told her to watch me and stay on her cell phone. Bob went across the street to his neighbor, Skip Stovall, who was working on a four-wheel ATV. He told Skip what was going on and asked him to help rescue me. They took Bob's pontoon boat down to the same ramp where I launched my boat. The battery on the boat was dead so they had to use his truck battery. By the time they reached me a good twenty-five to thirty minutes had passed. I was so stiff from the cold, I could not climb on board by myself, so they had me get on a small landing on the end of the boat and they rolled me on board like a log. All I could manage to do was to crawl to the middle of the boat and collapse. My boat was still going in tight circles but had slowed down considerably because it had been filling with water. I suggested they throw their anchor into my boat and try dragging it over to them. They succeeded on the first throw, and my boat careened into theirs and the engine died. It was so full of water that Skip had to climb into the boat and using a five-gallon bucket bailed out almost fifty gallons of water.

Towing my boat back to the ramp, Bob's wife met us at the ramp with a bunch of towels. As I dried off the best I could, they loaded up my boat for me, and I was soon on my way home.

When I got home and entered the house, I told my wife what had happened, but she was still giving me the silent treatment, which I am sure I deserved. For a split second I had the terrible feeling I was really dead and that she could not hear me or see me! Like shades of the movie, *The Sixth Sense,* I was scared out of my wits. Linda finally realized just how serious the situation had been and hurried me off to the shower.

When I finally realized I wasn't going to be in the obituaries, I started shivering violently and took a hot shower at Linda's insistence. I was still shivering four hours later. We went and bought a couple of gift certificates to a really fine steakhouse in Rockwall for Skip and Bob, and I bought a gift certificate for new towels for Bob's wife. Years later when I was the municipal development director for the City of Terrell, Bob came in to pull building permits to build a new Subway sandwich store. I introduced him to all of my staff and recalled the story of Bob and Skip saving my life that day.

I first heard the testimony of Carl Alsobrook and Jesse Vaughn in person at an employee-only conference for the City of Lancaster at Cedar Valley Community College in 2018 just after this miracle occurred. I was acquainted with Carl for a number of years before all this occurred, as the city manager in Royse City where I currently live. I had not met Jesse before he gave his testimony with Carl in 2018. Carl was kind enough to send me the *YouTube* video of their testimony so I could capture the essence of the miracle they experienced. With Carl's blessing I am including their testimony here in this book.

The story of how they met or even happened get to know each other is a testament of how God orchestrates our lives unbeknownst to us years in advance in order to show His power and glory to our benefit at the appointed time. When Jesse first started working in Royse City, Carl was the chief of police, so encountering each other during their routine business activities was highly unlikely. However, when Carl was promoted to the city manager's job only one position separated them, and that was the Community Development Corporation (CDC) director.

You would never know by looking at Jesse that he had stage five kidney failure as he played basketball and went jogging nearly every day. However, the doctors diagnosed him with kidney failure and immediately placed him on a donor's list where he languished for years without a single match. In the six years they had been acquainted, Carl and Jesse had only spoken to each other once. Carl said, "I heard you were the financial advisor around town and when I get done with some things, I am going to come to you with some money." Five years passed, and Carl never brought up the subject of money again. Jesse jokes that he thought Carl didn't like him because he never talked to him or inquired about finances.

Carl heard of Jesse's predicament and after some intense prayer decided to donate one of his kidneys to Jesse if they had a positive match. Carl would often swing past the board-room of the CDC to score some leftover donuts that were often available after the meeting. Normally, Jesse would leave the meeting immediately after it adjourned, but this one time he stayed to talk to the director. By that two- or three-minute delay, Carl and Jesse's paths were to cross *inadvertently* in the hallway. Coincidence, right? Carl told Jesse that he had something personal to discuss with him. The first thing to pop into Jesse's mind was it was about time Carl wanted to discuss his money situation. Jesse began to think this was really strange as Carl hardly ever said anything to him and wondered where the conversation was leading. Carl said, "I know there are HIPAA laws and such, and I don't want to be offensive, but I heard about your condition, and I would like to donate one of my kidneys to you." *HIPAA laws?* Jesse thought to himself, "There are no HIPAA laws in finance!" Jesse was so taken aback by Carl's statement that he reacted with complete stunned silence. About a week went by before Jesse called Carl to his office. Jesse thought, *"Now why would this guy offer his kidney to me?"*

Jesse finally realized the offer wasn't about him but was about God using Carl and him to show people God was still in the miracle business. Jesse stated that the experience just humbled him, at that point and he had to change his mind set about everything. "I realized He chose me. Why me? Why little ol' me? I'm just an ordinary person." Both Carl and Jesse realized God started to line things up from day one. Jesse recalls that when his company first said they were sending him to Royse City in 2011, he responded, *"No way!"* He had aspirations of being in a high-rise office building in downtown Dallas.

When Carl started to be tested for being a donor match, he was nearly fifty years old. Not only was he the same blood type, but his blood vessels were plaque free, and his heart was in perfect health but chemically his blood was like an eighteen-year-old—in spite of raiding the conference room of donuts.

Carl said, "When the doctor says a procedure might be a bit uncomfortable, he really means it is going to hurt like hell." He was required to take a twenty-four-hour urine test to determine the efficiency of the kidney function. The doctors told him that the target for a viable donor is 96 percent efficiency. After the surgery, the kidney would be expected to grow another 30 percent, so hopefully the end result would be greater than 70 percent, which should be sufficient to survive until age eighty-two.

The twenty-four-hour urine test is guaranteed to make you a public spectacle because everyone seems to know what the cooler and red sample bottle are for. When the results came back from the first test, they told Carl he would have to repeat the test. Then when he was told he had to take the test a third time, he exclaimed, "This is ridiculous, I know I'm not dumb enough to flunk a pee test!" The nurse explained that the first test came back at 210 percent efficiency, so everyone thought it must have been a mistake. The second test came back at 220 percent, and the third test scored 230 percent! The day before the surgery Carl's kidneys tested a whopping 242 percent. Carl's remaining kidney after surgery is operating at over 157 percent and Jesse's kidney function went from 5 percent to over 120 percent!

Jesse commented, "Just because I now have a white man's kidney in my black body, it isn't about race, it isn't about political unrest, it is about love, and we are all brothers and sisters in Christ." Carl regularly gets teased about his favorite health food diet—chili dogs with extra chili. Carl even has gotten Jesse to start eating chili dogs. It's a friendship brought together by Christ that will last a lifetime.

The next story comes from a dear friend and professional colleague, Terry Welch, one of premier planning attorneys in the State of Texas. My first contact with Terry was when I attended the University of Texas at Arlington for my master's degree in City and Regional Planning. Terry taught law classes at the annual American Planning Association (APA) conference that were required for my certification with the American Institute of Certified Planners (AICP). As one of the founding partners of Brown and Hofmeister Law Firm, teaching planning law was a natural extension of his already-prestigious career. We have worked together serving numerous small municipalities in all facets of land use and development. Our latest collaboration comes at the City of Wilmer in southern Dallas County, which, like many other small communities in North Texas, is experiencing growing pains. As a novice writer, I am in no position to improve on Terry's prose and at the risk of clumsy embellishment I will include Terry's story just as it was written for me to include in this collection of miracles.

God's Healing Powers, in Terry Welch's own words:

"I was blessed growing up by having a twin brother, Tim. While we had the usual brother fights and disagreements over the years, particularly as little kids, Tim was always my best friend. We had the same group of friends during our school years, shared a bedroom, enjoyed bothering our little sister, Laura, and helped each other with school work. All in all, pretty typical stuff growing up in a close family.

"Although I do not remember the exact date, sometime during our freshman high school year, Tim had been involved in a sporting activity at school. The following day, Tim did not feel well, and I thought perhaps he had a bug of some sort and was feeling under the weather. During the school day, he went to the nurse's office, and she called our father for him to pick Tim up from school to see a doctor. That was the extent of what was told to me, and I continued on with my school day. I got home later in the afternoon and Tim was not at home. I assumed that he was still at the doctor's office with Dad.

"By early evening, Laura and I were concerned because neither of our parents nor Tim was home yet, and since this was not an era where anyone had cell phones, we were waiting for a call or some type of update. We did not have to wait long before our parents got home, and we asked, "where's Tim?" Dad informed us that he had just come from the hospital, that Tim had been admitted, our mother was spending the night with him at the hospital, and Tim was going to have surgery early the following day. Both Laura and I were shocked to hear this. While I thought that perhaps Tim had a stomach bug of some sort, the doctor had examined him and determined that he had a hernia in his lower abdomen. While I wasn't too sure what exactly that meant, my father told us that there had been a tear in his abdomen wall and part of his small intestine had 'poked through' the abdomen wall. According to our family doctor, this was a very serious situation that necessitated surgery immediately, and that the failure to do so could result in Tim's death. X-rays and other scans had been performed at the hospital and confirmed the hernia. Tim was resting at the hospital. He had been sedated so that he would sleep and not move around, and surgery was scheduled for early the next morning. As a family, we prayed for Tim's healing.

"Dad left the house very early the next morning. Laura and I were instructed to go to school as usual, and Mom or Dad would contact us at school to give us an update. By 1:30 p.m. when I got home from school, I had not heard from my parents about Tim's condition. When I walked in the front door of our house, I was shocked to see Tim and both of my parents sitting in the living room. It was as though nothing had happened! Needless to say, I asked what was going on. They explained to me that when the doctors did some additional scans that morning in preparation for surgery, there was no abdominal wall tear, no part of his small intestine was protruding through the abdominal wall, and Tim felt fine. The doctors continued to do additional testing, but no issues were found, and Tim ultimately was released from the hospital.

"The doctors told my parents and Tim that they could not explain the change in his condition, and while they were apparently hesitant to term it a miracle, we knew that God has answered our prayers and had healed Tim. How else could you explain multiple X-rays and scans that showed a serious hernia condition one afternoon, and twelve hours later, everything was normal? Tim had no pain, could move around freely and the doctors concluded they might as well release him from the hospital and let him go home. He never had another issue with a hernia in his lower abdomen! God works miracles, and He heals people!"

This latest story is so recent that I had to hold up the final submission of the manuscript in order to get all the details. Tonya Thompson is the wife of Linda's cousin, Terry Thompson, who is Linda's father's sister's son. In August of 2021, Tonya started feeling very tired and by October the pain in her upper abdomen, and the swelling in her legs and feet was so severe it made it near impossible to do ordinary housekeeping and cooking. She had to take breaks every few minutes. Tonya was very reluctant to go to the doctor and just thought with home remedies, supplements, and good nutrition, it would resolve itself. By the first of November, she had been unemployed for nine months due to a lay off. But by the second week of November, Tonya got a job offer to start work November 29, 2021. By this time, breathing had become very difficult and her upper abdomen hurt so bad she had to sleep in a sitting position, and over-the-counter medicines did not alleviate the pain at all. Nothing worked.

Instead of going to work on the 29th of November, Tonya went to the ER and was admitted to the hospital. Due to all of the Covid-19 protocols, she had to sit in the emergency room waiting area for seven hours before finally being seen by a doctor. Her husband, Terry, was not even allowed to stay with her in the waiting room. After performing X-rays and a CT scan, the doctor came in with the bad news, she was given a diagnosis of cancer. They weren't sure what kind exactly at that time, but further diagnosis confirmed it to be Stage 4 Mantle Cell Lymphoma. Upon hearing the news, she declared in a prayer, "I will live and not die!" Tonya felt she should go through treatment even though she swore she would never put herself through that, especially, after seeing what it did to some of her family and friends. The enemy is a liar and comes only to steal, kill and destroy. Tonya declares through the Holy Spirit, "You have to make up your mind you are going to live and not die." The scripture from *2 Timothy 1:10* taken from the *Passion Translation* hit so close to home in Tonya's heart, it was as if the Holy Spirit was speaking directly to her about what God was about to do. Notice in the verse that Jesus dis-**mantled** death, a direct reference to the disease, **mantle** cell lymphoma.

*This truth is now being unveiled by the revelation of the anointed Jesus, our life-giver, who has **dismantled** death, obliterating all its effects on our lives, and has manifested his immortal life in us by the gospel. (**2 Timothy 1:10 The Passion Translation (TPT), Broad Street Publishing Group, LLC 2022.**)*

The pain continued to be so severe, the nurses had to administer pain medications through an IV, because pills were too slow. After three days in the hospital, they discharged her. On Friday, December 3, 2021, the pain in her abdomen was relentless and she finally took oxycodone pill to try to ease the pain. Later, she felt the pain start moving up from her lower abdomen to her chest and she sat up on the edge of the bed and the pain continued up her body and finally exited through the top of her shoulders! It took a minute for her to realize, but the pain was gone never to return– to this day, she is pain free! She describes this as her first miracle.

However, fluid continued to build up in the lining of her lungs and from November 2021 to February 2022, a total of ten, separate Thoracentesis procedures were performed where a long needle had to be inserted into the lower part of the lung's lining to remove the fluid. It had become so abnormally frequent, the doctors recommended a 'permanent' catheter be installed to drain the fluid, but she refused. It was not only going to be a major nuisance, but severely uncomfortable. She also felt in her spirit, it was not the direction to go. Enter the prayer warriors from her family, church (including a couple nurses), and friends from around the world. They would tell Tonya that the Holy Spirit had revealed to them very specific things they were to intercede on her behalf for. A P.E.T. scan revealed the cancer had metastasized to every lymph node in her body (from her chin to her upper leg area). Although she shared her illness with her circle of prayer warriors, she did not share this on social media and kept her battle private for the most part. They didn't need or want sympathy or people 'praying' who would not be praying or believing according to the promise and provision of Jesus Christ for our healing. They needed people who would pray and decree the Word, listen and pray according to the leading of Holy Spirit, and believe with her for the complete healing Jesus paid for. What He willingly gave wasn't going to be in vain!

Initially, Tonya's treatment was supposed to be chemical infusions every three weeks, but the chemical infusion the first weekend of January, caused extremely adverse effects and put her in the hospital for two weeks. It had gotten to the point where she couldn't walk without help, couldn't shower standing up, or do anything else without help. After all that, she told the Doctor she wasn't going to live in the hospital and keep dealing with these extreme side effects, so her Doctor changed the treatment protocol and switched her to a chemo pill that was taken twice a day. It's very important to note that every medication or transfusion of any kind was covered in prayer and the blood of Jesus. The chemo pill was no different – it was taken twice a day, so it was prayed over twice a day. Communion was also a normal part of prayer throughout this process. It was during this prayer time, the Holy Spirit started impressing on her that God did not need this pill to heal her. So, she started praying, "Lord, if you don't need this pill, just cause it to go straight through, from one end to the other. But then Holy Spirit strongly impressed upon her again that God did not need this pill to heal her. So, she quit taking it, and all the other prescription medications.

After refusing the catheter and other recommendations, the Doctor predicted dire consequences if she didn't take his advice and the medications as prescribed. The disease would return, become worse and render the medications ineffective. Her response was, "I know man can't heal me, but I know God can. I know what He has already healed me of, freed me from, and delivered me from!" She went on to share how she knew the Lord was faithful and trustworthy, and that nothing was too difficult for Him!

Between the end of November and the middle of February, it was estimated that 30-35 pounds of fluid (approximately 15 liters) had been removed from her lungs Around the first of March, not only was she pain free, but the swelling in her legs and feet completely subsided, her strength had returned, and the fluid buildup in her lungs had completely stopped building up, which baffled the nurses and doctors! She was able to cook, do the household chores again, stand and shower by herself, walk without assistance, and even climb stairs!

Tonya told her husband about the lies of the enemy coming against everything she knew to be true about her healing. First, because it is important to protect the promises and provision of the Lord working in our lives. Second, it is necessary to expose the enemy and suck the wind out of his sails by making his attacks and lies known. Tonya said, "When we bear one another's burdens and come into agreement with the Word of God, the promises of God, and the provision made by Jesus Christ through the spilling of His blood, the finished work of the Cross, and the power of the Resurrection Life, we wield the power and authority to overcome and be victorious!"

Tonya describes Terry as her true 'Knight in Shining Armor' and his constant support and love was and is invaluable and immeasurable. Their partnership in the Lord has defeated the enemy, overcome major obstacles, and seen victory after victory in their 23 years together.

As of this publication, Tonya is apparently cancer free and symptom free and death has indeed been dismantled!

THE ELEPHANT IN THE ROOM

I am still dumbfounded and at loss for words, whenever I try to understand why God spared my children and even my life and yet others have suffered horrible tragedies. I am so thankful God would give me another chance to get it right. It is such a terrible catastrophe to lose the most precious thing we have in this world, our children. Because my children were given such a wonderful gift of life, I cannot pretend I understand the grief of a parent who has lost a child. All I can do is grieve with them and love on them as a fellow parent who loves their own children. May God bring them a double portion of comfort and peace. I must say, however, I have learned to trust God implicitly no matter what the enemy throws at me.

I know what many of you are thinking right now. What about the miracles that did not happen, where there is no apparent happy ending? I think this question has been plaguing mankind from the beginning of time. This is the 'elephant in the room.' How could God let a precious little innocent child die from such a horrible disease as cancer or why was someone's wife was killed when the car skidded out of control on a patch of black ice or any number of other senseless tragedies? So many people have fallen away from the faith because these unexplainable calamities have put a wall between them and God. They shut God out of their lives because of unanswerable questions. It seems there will never be any satisfactory answers to the question of why a loving God would allow such things to occur.

I am no different in that regard and I have no answers from a human perspective. My faith in God is not based on my perception of why God acts or doesn't act in a particular situation. It is based on the fact that a real Jesus came to earth, suffered and died upon the cross in my stead and rose from the dead on the third day. In this and this alone, do I base all of my faith on.

In the case of a drunk driver, terrorist attack or a murder by a serial killer, we have a clear choice on who to blame—some obviously evil menace to society. When we have no clear idea who is responsible, we have the only too human reaction of blaming God for being unjust, unfair, uncaring, unloving, or unable to help.

No matter how much we suffer on this earth, God has given us away out. Like the words of the familiar hymn, "*When we have been there ten thousand years,*" will we even remember the suffering? Will we still blame God? Will we ask God the same questions, "Why my child? Why my wife? Why me?" The biggest part of faith is when we have more questions than answers, we just have to trust God. Satan's ultimate plan is to separate us from God, to wound us and harm us so that we blame God rather than the enemy. Jesus said these words, "Satan has come to steal, kill, and destroy. But I have come to give you life and that more abundantly."

The longest line in heaven will probably be that of those seeking answers. However, I suspect that line will only be filled with newcomers. They won't stay in line long, considering the incredible nature of heaven and the loving nature of God, that those in the line will simply realize that their questions are irrelevant and that there are better things to do in heaven than question God why.

Forgive me if I digress for a moment. There are some people, and not just a few, who don't value life as they ought. What about those who do not love their babies enough to spare their lives? I would be amiss if I didn't call out abortion for what it is—infanticide, genocide, or even murder. I am sure there are those out there who try to justify it based on rape or incest. However, look at the real statistics. Those cases are so infinitesimal they are not even statistically significant. I can't help but make a comparison of our culture to the worshippers of the ancient Baals who sacrificed their children with the most horrific painful method imaginable, by fire!

Billy Graham once stated that if God doesn't judge this country for its abortions, He would owe an apology to Sodom and Gomorrah! You can't sugarcoat this issue by hiding under the guise of 'legal' abortion. John Lennox in an interview on *Socrates in the City* with Eric Metaxas made the clearest case against abortion I have ever heard, "The left calls a fetus just a blob of undifferentiated tissue, but that tissue will develop into a living, breathing human being; it will not become a dog or a cat or a fish but a living human being created in the image of God. Who gave *you* the authority to interfere or destroy something made in the image of God?" What capital crime has a baby committed that is deserving of a death sentence? None.

Make no mistake God will hold us accountable for over sixty million deaths of innocent unborn babies. Twelve times the number of innocent Jews killed by Hitler in the Holocaust!

We can only hope and pray this country repents and bans abortion in the near future. As Christians, we must step up to the plate and raise our children and bring them up as the Bible commands.

> *Fathers, do not provoke your children to anger, but bring them up in the discipline and instruction of the Lord.* **(Eph. 6:4)**

Someone said if heaven were on earth, none of us would ever want to go to heaven. Since, we live in a fallen world, we should expect bad things to happen. It is not God's fault, and you certainly can't blame God for the bad things that do happen. We are the ones to blame. We did this to ourselves. It is called free choice. If God chose to fix everything so that we didn't suffer any consequences, He would have to remove our free will and with it the ability to experience love, emotions, reason, imagination, choices, art, beauty, and freedom. Enforced love is not love at all; it would just be a robotic response.

An atheistic scientist has said, "We are just 'dancing' to our DNA." That is not my idea of love. It has to be freely given from a free will. God cannot make us love Him. As the result of having the free choice of loving God also comes the choice of rejecting Him. God doesn't send anyone to hell—we send ourselves.

So, when suffering or tragedy strikes, I know that God still loves us no matter what, and nothing can ever separate us from the love of God. If we just persevere and stay the course and run the race and finish well, the momentary sting of suffering here on earth will rapidly fade when we get to the other side. That is our hope, and the only real choice we have is to trust in Jesus with all our hearts. I know this is true because "I have seen too much!"

MY GREAT CLOUD
OF WITNESSES

I have a circle of friends, most who are long-time friends and mostly colleagues and all devout men of God. I call them my 'great cloud of witnesses.' They have all been a tremendous encouragement to me over the years, and some of the most remarkable miracles I have ever witnessed involves them. There is Andrew Seigrist, David Denney, Lawrence Crow, Jerry Sparks, Ricky Mendez, Dwight Lancaster, Steve Dake, Terry Welch, and Jeff Odell. Some have already gone on to be with the Lord. I am sure there are many others that have boosted my faith over the years that I have lost count. I guess as I recall them, I will make note to continue this book in a sequel someday. Isn't that the way Hollywood works, to have the sequel planned even before the original movie debuts?

> *Therefore, since we have so great a cloud of witnesses surrounding us, let us also lay aside every encumbrance and the sin which so easily entangles us, and let us run with endurance the race that is set before us.+* ***(Heb. 12:1)***

A word about David Denney, it is not really about miracles but about his faith. He was one of my building inspectors when I took over as the director in 2007 in Terrell. I soon recognized an extraordinary level of both competence and ethical standards in him. I promoted him to building official the following year.

David was in his early fifties, and when he went in for routine checkup, they discovered what the doctor thought was just a cyst on his back. However, when they lanced it, no fluids came out, which surprised the doctor. Upon performing a biopsy, they discovered it was melanoma and subsequently removed it, thinking they had gotten it all. Instead when the pathology report came back, it was not growing from the outside in but was growing from the inside out. Further tests revealed it was in his lungs, spine, brain, and other organs and tissues. The cancer was inoperable, but they tried a new laser treatment so accurate it could zap a single cancer cell, and combined with an experimental drug that cost $10,000 a month, promised to give him a fighting chance.

When all of his sick leave ran out, he was forced to take medical retirement, and as result, his insurance lapsed for only about a month. The cancer was so aggressive that it came storming back. He told me that the only thing he was worried about was how his family would fare without him. It was such a blessing that he was able to see his youngest daughter married. I never once heard him complain about the terrible pain he suffered and never heard him utter any regrets. I have never witnessed such stalwart faith in anyone I have ever known. To say he finished the race well is an understatement.

Before he got sick, he was nominated for Code Professional of the Year in the State of Texas, and Lawrence Crow presented the award to David at a City Council meeting in Terrell. Later, on his deathbed, Lawrence nominated David to be awarded the title of Honorary Certified Building Official (CBO) by the International Code Council out of Washington, DC. The ICC develops and publishes all of the International Building Codes used throughout the United States. David received this recognition posthumously.

I can only hope that I can demonstrate such bravery, such faith, in the face of death as David did. David went home to the Lord on Sunday January 4, 2015. Lawrence Crow, Jerry Sparks, Andrew Seigrist, Jeff Odell, and Dwight Lancaster and many others were real prayer warriors throughout David's heroic battle with cancer.

I met first met Lawrence Crow and Jerry Sparks when I became city arborist for the City of Irving in the Building Inspections Department in March 2000. I really didn't remember when I first met them, so I cheated and peeked at my old resume. If I had not recorded these events in my prayer journal right after they happened, I don't think I would have remembered them as clearly as I do. But it seems like it was just yesterday that the events happened, so indelibly are they etched into my memory. My memory on most things is so bad that I often joke about if I ever get Alzheimer's disease, no one will be able to tell the difference.

When Lawrence had first moved to Irving he worked in the private sector and as a construction superintendent and later supervised the construction of the Exxon World Headquarters before becoming a building inspector for the City of Irving. I'll let you get to know Jerry better in a moment. The time was before cell phones and GPS, and Lawrence had gone before his family to rent a house in Irving. His wife, Teresa, was instructed to leave Abilene in West Texas early enough to get to Irving before dark, and as it happened, as it so often does in the words of Robert Burns: "the best laid plans of mice and men go awry."

After a late start, she and their two boys arrived after dark and missed a critical turn, and it soon became apparent that she was hopelessly lost. The boys soon picked up on the anxiety of their mom and were soon crying. At around 10 p.m., after driving aimlessly around without finding a familiar street, Teresa spotted a lone porch light on at the end of a cul-de-sac. Out of desperation, she decided to knock on the door. A woman answered the door and asked Teresa if she needed help. Teresa explained that her husband had rented a house, and she couldn't find it and was completely lost. The lady asked what the address was, and when Teresa told her what the address was, she was so shocked that she asked Teresa to repeat it. The lady replied, "Of course I know where it is. I'm your landlord!" You are never lost to God. God not only knows where you are at all times, He even knows how many hairs are on your head. In my case, it doesn't take very long to count mine these days. This incident is a crystal-clear demonstration of how God has your back. You just don't get a busy signal when you call out His name.

When you drill down to the truth about God, it is a very humbling realization that the God of the entire universe cares enough about us as individuals and loves us beyond understanding to care about even the little things in our everyday lives. He cares about even things only we care about or have meaning only to us. Jesus has our back! If anyone desires to know Jesus all they have to do is turn around and He will be found right behind you with His arms wide open. God is never too busy or so far above the fray that He ignores our cries for help *(Deut. 31:8)*.

Now Jerry Spark's story. He also worked for the City of Irving in the Inspections Department with Lawrence and me. Jerry was a mechanical systems inspector, air conditioning and heating to the uninitiated. Hold onto your seat because this story will blow your socks off. If it doesn't, you need to go to the emergency room and have them check for a pulse. This event actually started on my birthday, February 8, 2014, when Jerry came home from the store to their home on Cedar Creek Reservoir, located about fifty miles southeast of Dallas. When he got home, he discovered his wife, Alice, lying in the front doorway unconscious.

The ambulance rushed her to local hospital in Gun Barrel City where they thought she had suffered a heart attack. They didn't have a cardiologist on duty, so they decided to care flight Alice to the hospital in Athens, Texas. After arriving there, the doctors could not even register her brain waves, much less find a pulse. The doctors, including both a cardiologist and a neurologist, were both doing everything they could to revive her. In time, Jerry's pastor and most of his family arrived and started a prayer vigil.

So, after conducting extensive tests on Alice they finally declared her officially deceased, and the attending doctor signed her death certificate. The doctor asked Jerry if they had considered donating her organs, and Jerry answered in the affirmative. One of his sons was coming from a long distance away, and he had asked his father, Jerry, that nothing be done until he got there. They kept Alice on a life-support machine during the night in order to preserve her organs with the intention of taking some of her organs the next day.

They held the prayer vigil all through the night, and in the morning, Jerry signed the consent forms to donate her organs.

At around 9 a.m., the staff wheeled her body up to the surgery room and a nurse came in to prep the body for surgery. She started by stuffing a large wad of cotton in Alice's mouth, and at that instant Alice opened her eyes, spit the cotton out, and shouted, "*What are you doing to me*?" The nurse screamed and ran from the room. The nurse called Jerry immediately, extremely agitated and said, "You need to talk to the doctor right away," and 'click' she hung up. A few moments later the doctor called and in a very calm voice told Jerry, "You wife, Alice, is all right!" Jerry replied, "What do you mean? Is she wiggling her toes or something?" "No, she is sitting up and talking to the nurses!"

I defy anyone to try to explain this by any medical means known to man. This was a genuine miracle of 'biblical' proportions, no ifs, ands, or buts. But that is not the end of the story. Several months later, they sold their house on Cedar Creek Lake and were planning to buy a house in the resort community of Hot Springs Village in Arkansas. As the day for closing approached, his mortgage company called and said there was problem with his credit and the loan was about to be denied. Jerry told them that his credit was perfect, but upon investigation he found out that the insurance company had refused to pay for Alice's hospital visit. Their reason, "We don't cover dead people!" Jerry had to call the hospital president and explain what had happened, and the hospital administrator had to get a court order to rescind the death certificate before the loan would go through.

The following Monday, Jerry called me to let me know what had transpired over the weekend. I made the remark, "I bet you guys are going to have a pretty special Valentine's Day, huh!" After they got settled in at Hot Springs Village, Linda and I went up and visited them at their new home. Alice says she doesn't recall any of it. There were no visions of heaven and no light at the end of a tunnel or any of the popular near-death experiences. It is chilling to think that the surgery to retrieve her organs might have been completed before she regained consciousness.

Ironically, Jerry died a few years later. At his funeral, both Lawrence and I got to talk to Alice, and she looked unbelievably well considering what had happened to her.

Jeff Odell has an incredible story to tell about his grandson, who is now a rambunctious two-year-old. Jeff is a rock-solid Christian of the first degree. He and I get together once in a while for lunch, and we are always sending encouraging text messages back and forth. Come to think of it, right now I need to get together with him soon; I could sure use an encouraging word. I have known Jeff for over twenty-five years, and during that time, his faith has never faltered. I have to confess if it were not for being surrounded by this great cloud of witnesses, I know I would not have the faith I have today. I cannot empha-size enough the importance of having strong and reliable prayer partners who come along side in any situation.

It started out as a typical routine pregnancy for Mia, Jeff's daughter-in-law, and the birth was expected to be smooth and without complications. Upon discovering the baby was a boy, they decided to call him Elliot. When the time came to take Mia to the hospital, Jeff was still at work, and he told his son J. C. to go ahead and go to the hospital because it was raining and just keep them posted. Because the onset of the labor was taking a little longer than expected and Mia's blood pressure started to increase, the doctors decided to induce labor by rupturing the amniotic sac, commonly called water breaking. That's when things took a turn for the worse. The placenta was inadvertently cut, causing the blood supply to the baby's brain to be interrupted for several crucial minutes. At this point a surgeon was called in to perform an emergency caesarean section.

When little Elliot was finally delivered, he was not breathing on his own, and the situation quickly turned critical. The result of being deprived of oxygen, Elliot was what is known as a 'blue baby.' They put him on a ventilator and placed him in the NICU unit with around-the-clock monitoring. The doctor came and got J.C. from the waiting room, who was wondering why everything was taking so long. Instead of taking him to Mia's room, he ushered him into a small conference room where the doctor explained what happened and the dire prognosis. The doctor painted a very grim picture. The doctor said it was so serious they might even lose Elliot.

After an MRI was performed, large portions of his brain showed up as dark areas on the images, showing oxygen deprivation, and the doctor told J. C. to prepare for the worst. Elliot would likely have palsy (paralysis from brain damage) and other debilitating complications. Elliott was placed on life-support equipment for the night. When Jeff and his wife, Sheila, received the devastating news, Jeff pleaded with God not to take little Elliot home. Jeff told his son, J. C. and daughter-in-law, Mia, that the situation was beyond what the doctors could do, and it was in God's hands. He told them, "If you don't know how, it is time to learn to talk to God. Learn to trust God."

The doctors induced a coma to give the brain a chance to recover. For the next month they kept him in the coma, and it was in this condition Jeff saw his grandson for the first time. At least he wasn't born prematurely and weighed a healthy seven and a half pounds. Elliot was kept in the NICU unit for a total of thirty-four days, which stretched through Christmas and New Year's Day.

Finally, they took him off the ventilator, and he began breathing on his own. The doctor started to slowly bring him out of the coma. The family was summoned, and they were told they could briefly hold Elliott. When they got to the room, the nurse was already holding him and said to Jeff, as he entered the room, "I am a Christian, and I just knew there was just something about this baby." The next day Elliot opened his eyes for the first time, and it was a moment of great rejoicing for the whole family.

The doctors performed another MRI and the dark areas had all disappeared. The doctor admitted he was utterly astonished. After a few more precautions, they released them all to go home. Like I said in the opening statement, Elliot is a normal, thriving, energetic two-year-old today.

That brings me to Dr. Andrew Seigrist who is a school superintendent down on the Texas coast. I have known Andrew since 2003, and we have been prayer partners for over nineteen years! We pray together at least a couple of times a month, sometimes even more. We are available to each other any time day or night. Just a text of '911' gets a response within minutes. We started out as fishing buddies on the *Lake Lavon Fishing Forum*. Shortly after I nearly drowned, Andrew was kind enough to buy my aluminum fishing boat. He has three children, Adam the oldest, Nathan, and Caitlin, his youngest daughter. I have witnessed his kids grow up, go off to college, and watched as they grew their wings and moved off on their own. Adam is now enrolled in seminary, Caitlin is finishing up college and is now engaged, and Nathan is a newlywed. I am almost as proud of his kids as I am of my own.

We are always sharing our burdens with each other like this note in my prayer journal, dated October 2, 2014. Andrew shared with me that morning that there were a lot of worrisome things going on in his life, and I later sent a text of a scripture I heard on the radio that day was **Proverbs 12:25:** *"Anxiety in the heart of a man weighs it down, but a good word makes it glad."* After Andrew responded, I texted Andrew, "You have made my heart glad today, brother!" Andrew texted back thanks for sharing and encouraging him.

It was in the spring of 2016, and the crappie fishing was at its peak. Andrew and I hired a guide, Jerry Hancock, for a day of fishing on Lake Lavon. Jerry took us to his favorite spots without much luck, so we decided pull in close to the dam and try fishing off the rocks. My first cast netted a nice crappie. Jerry kept tabs of how many we caught with a little push button counter he called his 'tally whacker.' He even counted the ones we later threw back after our limit was reached, and we swapped them for bigger ones. When all was said and done, Jerry had tallied 153 crappies.

Hmmm. Where have I heard that number before—maybe *John 21:11?* I have no doubt that was best day fishing Peter and company ever had. Likewise, Andrew and I had the best day fishing ever before or since. In another bit of "coincidence," this occurred on Good Friday.

It is often in the midst of tragedy that our faith is tested the hardest. It is at times like these that having faithful prayer partners mean the most. On January 30, 2015, I was startled awake at 5:30 in the morning. I was dreaming Andrew was saying, "Amen and Amen," which is how we always end our prayer sessions. I called Andrew around 8 a.m. as was our usual time and found out that one of his School Board Trustees was a volunteer fireman and had responded to no less than three fatality emergencies that weekend for the first time as a first responder.

Andrew stated that his small tight knit community sorely needed prayers as they were reeling from the tragedies. Then on the way to work, I heard on the radio that God prepares us just for times such as this when we need to be an encouragement to others. Andrew, by his faith and character, without hesitation stepped into the role of encouraging his community through this time of great need. Andrew literally prayed with these first responders as a body covered with a sheet lay nearby. Later, because of Andrew's leadership role as the community's prayer warrior, the volunteer fire department asked if he would be their chaplain, which he cherishes as a great honor *(Isa. 6:8)*.

Andrew and I, along with a myriad of others, have heard the voice of the Lord and said, "Send me." I praise God over and over for sending such faithful friends and prayer partners into my life. I am so thankful for people God has intentionally put in my path and the Holy Spirit has prompted me to pray for or speak to about Jesus. My life, such as it is, after nearly drowning, surviving cancer twice, and two strokes is the result, no doubt, of countless answered prayers. I don't always know who has been praying for me, but please, whoever you are, don't ever cease your prayers. I can certainly tell when someone has been praying for me.

I regret that over the years that I didn't record more answers to Andrew's and my prayers in my journal. There are so many more events I could have included in this book. One memorable incident I did record happened on the National Day of Prayer. Andrew and I had committed earlier to pray together on this auspicious day. We first opened the prayer as usual, praying for family and friends, and then turned to praying for our country which even to this day is in desperate need for prayer.

A special request had come up, and Andrew asked me to pray for the wife of a friend of his who had cancer. That afternoon she was to go in for a preop examination for surgery that was to occur the next morning. When the scans were completed, all the signs for this very advanced cancer were gone except a few small spots left on her lymph nodes, which were removed in the doctor's office, and she was sent home. At 4 p.m. that same day, Andrew called me back incredibly excited and told me I had to be the first to know about the answer to our prayers, and I am sure many other prayers on her behalf. The best news was that they cancelled the surgery scheduled for the following morning.

Just think of the volume of prayers sent that day because it was the National Day of Prayer, and God reached down to a miniscule little town on the Texas coast to answer this petition and cry for mercy. It has been so hard for me to write of these many stories of miracles without choking up all over again as they become fresh in my mind again, Hallelujah!

I have known Dwight Lancaster since I worked as an assistant city planner at the City of Wylie between 2001 and 2004. Dwight was one of the building inspectors and eventually became the building official before moving to the City of Canton as their building official. Dwight is a voracious reader of the Bible. He reads through the book of Proverbs every month, thirty-one chapters in thirty or thirty-one days, and has read the entire Bible so many times he has lost count. He is a true scholar and has so many versions and translations of the Bible. I don't think even *Amazon* can compete with his collection.

Dwight suffered a stroke several years ago, and it really curtailed his ability to read. No doubt, I repeat, no doubt this is the work of an enemy bent on keeping the Word of Truth from us. He has recovered now enough to resume his Bible scholarship. We now are engaged in spiritual warfare together in that almost every week we are praying for our country together through next November's election.

He recalls is a story of prophecy by his grandmother Lancaster, although none of the other family members recall the incident, which is understandable because it happened nearly ninety years ago. As the story goes Dwight's grandmother foretold of a great war that was coming even before the rumors of World War II started. She said her two sons would enlist in that war and would come home alive unharmed and would even run into each other while traveling from opposite ends of the world, all of which came to pass.

There are so many things now to pray for that it hard to decide what the priorities are. If you are reading this before November 2022, please join us in prayer. We need more than a National Day of Prayer; we need a National Year of Prayer. Let's put on the full armor of God and join the battle for the soul of America! It is easy to get discouraged with all that Christians see happening all around them on every side. There is strength in numbers, however. I heartily recommend surrounding yourself with faithful dedicated prayer partners as I have done. Instead of despair whenever I turn on the news, I feel hope that through prayer, we can beat back the forces of evil.

That's why I have included the *Barefoot Brigade* in this book. It is a clear path we can take to increase our effectiveness in this spiritual warfare we have found ourselves engaged in whether we like it or not.

Sometimes the spiritual warfare gets real, and it becomes a battle just to keep from being anxious and gripped by fear. Several years ago, Linda had to drive me to the emergency room at Baylor Hospital in Garland because I had a very painful bout with kidney stones. We even had to pull over once because I had a violent case of nausea on the way. A short time after we arrived, I was given some powerful pain medicine which did little to alleviate the pain. About 9:00 a.m., I was able to pass several stones naturally, and the sharp pains immediately subsided. The subsequent X-rays revealed that indeed the kidney stones were gone.

The emergency doctor came in and confirmed the crisis was over and that she was going to go ahead and sign the discharge papers. As she left the room, she suddenly turned and said, "By the way, there is a spot on your kidney." She had no further explanation and just left me wondering what that was supposed to mean. Before I even had a chance to say anything, the doctor disappeared and I never saw her again. It suddenly dawned on me that this was an insidious lie from the enemy designed to cause fear. I doubt very seriously that the doctor even realized the implications of what she so nonchalantly said. I just knew that it was a spiritual issue and not a medical one. I heard the Holy Spirit quietly say, "Take the lie and get rid of it before it takes root."

I literally envisioned reaching my hand into my abdomen and grabbing what appeared to be a small octopus and pulling it out, I made a throwing motion toward the wall of the exam room. I could almost hear the wet splatting sound as it hit the wall and slid to the floor. Convinced I had halted the lie in its tracks, I never thought about it again. By 3 p.m. I began wondering why they were taking so long to discharge me, so I called my wife to pick me up, and I removed the IV from my arm, got dressed, made the bed and left the hospital.

On the way home the hospital called me on my cell phone and asked where I was. I stated, "I am on my way home." To which they exclaimed, "You can't do that!" I sarcastically replied, "What do you mean I can't do that? I just did!" The voice on the other end of the phone informed me that the insurance would not pay for my visit if I wasn't properly discharged. I said, "That sounds like your problem not mine." They hung up and called back a few minutes later and said everything had been taken care of and not to worry about a thing. By this time, I had on the full armor of God and I was itching for a fight.

About six years later, I had another bout with kidney stones, and I went to see my regular doctor in Terrell. After the X-rays were completed, he came in and said there were several large stones in my kidneys and suggested that my urologist perform a lithotripsy to pulverize the stones so I could pass them naturally. He then said, "By the way, there is a spot on one of your kidneys, and it appears to be simply a discoloration, a shadow if you will, and it is completely benign." I thanked the Holy Spirit for revealing the truth to me years before. It is important to listen not only to the small, still voice of God but the hissing sound of the devil whispering lies into your ear. Just say, "Bub, you don't belong in here, there is nothing you can do to shake my faith. I have seen too much, so get out of here, in the name of Jesus, Amen!"

MIRACLES CLOSER TO HOME

I told the story about Jerry's wife, Alice, at Easter in 2014, and it opened a whole new discussion about miracles that happened to Linda's side of the family. Linda's parents, Lelia and Cliff, became sweethearts at the ripe old age of six years old when Lelia gave Cliff a bag of candy, and they were inseparable for the rest of their lives. At age eight, Lelia contracted diphtheria, a disease that has been all but eradicated from the US, with only five cases reported since 2000. Lelia's father-in-law, known as Daddy Lemmonds, was a Pentecostal preacher, and when he prayed for Lelia's healing, all signs of the illness disappeared immediately.

Daddy Lemmonds was a true 'fire and brimstone' preacher, and Linda along with the rest of the kids in the family were often frightened by his fiery sermons. Later when Linda was dating Freddy Hill, who was to later marry her, Freddy and his future brother-in-law, Jerry, came to Daddy Lemmonds' church with Linda and her sister, Sharon. Daddy Lemmonds' sermon soon energized the congregation to such an extent that people began dancing and praising God in the aisles with uplifted hands. Freddy and Jerry had never before witnessed such an outpouring of the Holy Spirit, and when the joyous worship service reached a crescendo, they bolted upright and fled from the church. However, as many family members can attest, many answers to prayer came out of his pulpit, and I think the devil was downright afraid to enter his church.

Linda's father, Cliff, loved to cook and he prepared the meals at every church gathering for years and years. They even had a tradition every Monday that all the family and friends and sometimes even strangers would come over for dinner. Several years ago, for a Christmas present we put together an extensive family recipe book in which we gathered recipes from moms and dads, brothers and sisters, grandmothers and grandfathers, aunts and uncles, nieces and nephews and then matched up hundreds of family photos, especially humorous ones and then told the backstory behind each recipe. One was the picture we took of our two great-grandsons who jumped out of the kiddie pool stark naked and proceeded to pee on a tree. The caption read, "Beware of secret ingredients."

The idea began when our granddaughters started asking us to teach them how to cook. In the middle of the book we included a recipe called "*Mondays at Mother and Daddy's*," commemorating the wonderful traditions associated with gatherings around the dinner table. A foreshadow of the Marriage Feast of the Lamb no doubt.

As I mentioned earlier, Linda's mom and dad were very involved in their church. One summer in the early seventies, they decided to go with a church group to a retreat in the Ozark Mountains in northwestern Arkansas. There was a convoy of six cars in which Cliff and Lelia were in the second car from the lead. They were slowly winding their way through the mountains with a gorge dropping away precipitously to their left and steep cliffs to their right. Suddenly the lead car full of people veered off the road and started to fall into the ravine, much to the horror of those who were behind the lead car.

At that instant, those who were in the second and third cars in the line witnessed a giant hand reach down and catch the lead car, lifting it up back onto the roadway unharmed. The strange thing, if indeed that wasn't strange enough, the people in the lead car never saw the hand and only had the sensation of a large jolt before stopping on the road. The people in the second and third cars were so excited they were besides themselves, including Cliff and Lelia. The other cars were too far back and did not see the incident. They speculated that the driver must have fallen asleep, but that was never confirmed. In any case, they were all safe and sound. Lelia said of the incident later, "We had a revival right there in the middle of the road!"

My wife's aunt Betty was only four years old in 1948 when she experienced a remarkable miracle. One Sunday, she was walking the short distance to church with her parents when another church member offered Betty a ride in their car. As this was her first-ever ride in an automobile, she was very excited. When they arrived, Betty jumped out of the car to run back to where her parents were still walking. As Betty ran from between the parked cars, she was instantly struck by an oncoming car. The right headlight struck her in the head, knocking the light out and at the same time, fracturing her skull. Before the man could stop the car, it drove completely over Betty and the broken rear bumper guard that was hanging down caught her leg ripping it wide open.

The man who was driving the car that struck Betty emerged from the car completely hysterical as were the rest of the people who saw how badly she was injured. In the ensuing panic, a man who lived across the street, who witnessed the horrific accident, reached the scene and quickly said a prayer based on a Bible verse he said would stop the bleeding. No one remembers the scripture, but the results speak for themselves. Betty was put in a church member's car since an ambulance would take too long to arrive. It took nearly forty-five minutes to get to Parkland Hospital in Dallas. At that time, the old Parkland Hospital was located on Harry Hines Boulevard across the Trinity River from the church.

Because her leg was not bleeding when she arrived at the hospital, they assumed she was dead. One of the attending doctors, after examining the horrendous wound, determined that Betty couldn't be saved and just 'sewed her up for the funeral,' as the doctor put it and wheeled her gurney back into her hospital room. The following morning, the attending physician told the nurses to prepare Betty for transfer to the morgue. However, when they got to her room, she was still alive but was completely unconscious.

Betty remained unconscious for several days afterward, and when the nurses came into her room early the morning of the fourth day, Betty was sitting up with tears streaming down her face, not because of the pain, but because her mother had not yet arrived. Her mother had to walk a considerable distance to catch the bus, so it was late morning before she got to the hospital. When she finally got better, Betty remembers that the man who was driving the car brought her a very pretty frilly yellow dress. She completely recovered, albeit, with a long ugly scar on her leg.

Betty today is a devoted Christian and an avid reader of Christian literature. She shares our love of scholarly Bible study and even traveled with my wife and I to visit the *Ark Encounter* with the life-sized replica of Noah's ark located in northern Kentucky and the nearby *Creation Museum*. Today, we all attend church together at *Millwood Church,* a small country church in a tiny community, located at the intersection of two rural highways, called Union Valley. Pastor Kip Brockway is wonderfully Spirit-filled as are his messages. This small church has an international following online as far away as Ireland and Washington State. Pastor Kip has a Gospel rock band called, "*Stained Red,* that brings the Gospel to otherwise unreachable places. Please pray that this small congregation will continue to grow and increase our influence for the kingdom. Pray that Pastor Kip's music ministry will continue to share the Gospel and bring *light* into places of darkness.

The next one to share at our big Easter get together was Sondra, Linda's younger sister. In 2012, Sondra had fallen and fractured her wrist and went to an emergency clinic where they took X-rays of her hand and put a cast on her arm. The pain still persisted, even with the cast on, and she was prescribed some strong pain medicine to help dull the excruciating throbbing in her hand. The doctor put the X-rays up on a monitor and showed her the tiny white fractures on the screen. The doctor then burned a CD of the images and told her to take it to her orthopedic surgeon for treatment. When she got to the surgery center, they insisted that they take their own X-rays (everyone has to get piece of the insurance pie). When the X-rays were finished, the doctor had a puzzled look on his face. All of the fractures were gone, and the doctor stated he thought she had gotten the records of someone else, which Sondra denied emphatically, and she knew that a miracle had occurred because the pain had also disappeared. They took her cast off and sent her on her way. As with a lot of people, some doctors just 'know' too much to admit there are miracles. I guess medical school didn't teach them that miracles are not only possible, but more commonplace than you'd think. Maybe these doctors should be given some of their money back for gaps in their education.

FRUITS OF THE SPIRIT

I n what ways has witnessing so many miracles began to bear fruit in my life? The first evidence that comes to mind is what I described in the beginning of this book. My faith is visible to others, such as my grandkids who have asked me to baptize them and in the case of my grandson, Jacob, to officiate at his wedding. I don't think I intentionally try to wear my faith like some sort of gaudy shirt to attract attention to myself. Other true Christians understand exactly what I mean. Our joy in the Lord is spontaneous and is clearly visible to others, but unbelievers can sense our joy as well try to find fault in our character simply because they are incapable of understanding the source of our inward happiness.

Shortly after I took over as municipal development director in Terrell, I was able to hire a new code enforcement supervisor, Ricky Mendez. He is a man of impeccable work ethic and integrity and got things done to clean up the city that were considered to be impossible. We regularly conducted predevelopment meetings with developers, engineers, architects, contractors, and other professionals. Each department would usually send their department head or senior staff from each discipline. At these meetings, the developer would get details on what construction standards they would have to abide by and what submittals they were required to turn in with their applications for development permits. Ricky represented code enforcement, job site environmental controls, and housing.

A particular department head, who shall remain nameless, made it a point that he was in charge, and everything had to be done his way or it was the highway. This is commonly called 'Large and in Charge' or 'Little Man' syndrome. He deemed his job description was to set up roadblocks any way he could to hinder a project. I saw my job as a sort of a travel agent; you told me where you wanted to go, and I would help you get there. You can see that this led to obvious conflicts down the road. This particular person began taking cheap shots at me in front of other professionals every chance he got. I don't know where I got the strength to never retaliate in kind but just smiled and pretended not to understand the gist of what he was implying.

I retired in December 2015 and after three years of nearly starving as a consultant, I came out of retirement in 2018 to work for the City of Lancaster as their development services director. I caught up with my finances quickly and retired again after just a year and left Lancaster on January 31, 2019. The deputy city manager, Rona Stringfellow, also left the same day and took over as city administrator for nearby Wilmer. She immediately asked if I was interested in a part time consulting job as their city planner, I jumped at the chance, knowing I only had to work twenty hours a week, and that mostly from home. I guess by now you are wondering where all this is going and what it has to do with Ricky. Well, when I first hired Ricky some ten or eleven years earlier, I had hired him away from Lancaster where he worked for Rona! I strongly recommended that he be hired by Wilmer as their building official, which Rona subsequently did. Small world isn't it?

To bring it home full circle to Terrell and the fruits of the Spirit discussion, when Ricky came to work for Wilmer, we were reminiscing about Terrell, and he said, "In all the years I saw you take abuse at those meetings, I just couldn't believe you never once retaliated but just kept smiling." I had never thought much about it, but in hindsight, I thanked God the indwelling of the Holy Spirit who kept my testimony intact. Remember, the truth does not require anyone to believe in it to remain the truth. However, a lie must be believed to hold power. I think from a purely worldly view, I would been expected to fire off a few salvos, and nobody would probably blamed me for it. But for that fleeting moment of smug satisfaction, I would surely have lost the respect of the 'real' professionals in the room.

Rona Stringfellow is the best example I know of how a Christian ought to act in the workplace, especially as an executive in a governmental administration office. Her Bible is always is in plain view on her desk, and she is bold in her declaration of being a Christian, which it shows in her demeanor and actions. Yet, Rona doesn't have to tell anyone she is a Christian; it becomes self-evident rather quickly. She has allowed me to anoint her office doors with oil both in Lancaster and Wilmer with the following Psalm as the key scripture:

> *Open the gates of righteousness to me;*
> *I will enter through them, I will give thanks to the Lord.*
> *This is the gate of the Lord;*
> *The righteous will enter through it.*
> *I will give thanks to You, for You have answered me,*
> *And You have become my salvation. (Psalm 118:19–21)*

Have you ever noticed how you can sense a person is a Christian without them even saying a word? Rona is among the many people I have known who have a joy and peace that affects everyone around them. The Holy Spirit lives within all believers, and that Spirit agrees with your spirit. It is this very presence of the Holy Spirit that animates the enemy to attack us when we have done nothing wrong. I know that in Wilmer, I am in a safe working environment from a spiritual perspective.

When I had my first stroke back in November 2020, I was lying in bed with my door open to the hall of the hospital, and I noticed a man go past my doorway several times as if looking for someone or something. He didn't have a uniform on, so I didn't think he was a staff person. But there was something about his demeanor that was unmistakable, and you couldn't mistake that glow of joy about him. He passed by my door for the third time, and I was prompted by the Holy Spirit to say something, but my hesitance allowed him to keep going. So, I prayed, "Lord, send him back again." He immediately turned around and came back. When he paused again outside my door, I called out, "Now there goes a man with a prayer in in his heart!" He came into my room, and it was then I noticed his name tag, he was the hospital chaplain! We had a very lively discussion about our love of Jesus, and as he left my room he turned, and said. "Well, I've had my sermon for the day!"

Unfortunately, your Spirit of Truth draws its share of hate-filled people as well. As I thoroughly covered this earlier, I won't go into another diatribe about it. Suffice it to say, Jesus warned us about these people and said if they hated Him, they would surely hate us as well. I think if such a person comes out of their lair for a moment and just attacks you for no reason, you can wear that as a badge of honor. The spirit inside unsaved people can sense the Holy Spirit living within you, and sometimes they will attack you immediately when you have done or said nothing. It's not you but the Spirit within you that draws the attack of the enemy. You should actually consider thanking them for validating the faith inside you. Do you need some charcoal lighter for the coals you just heaped on their head?

I once was in line in the lobby of a McDonald's in Quinlan, Texas, one morning, and I ran into a kindred spirit I had met several months before, who had made it his mission to help veterans cut through the red tape to obtain their overdue benefits. In this case, he asked me if I had any prayer requests, and when I nodded yes, he didn't hesitate, and we prayed right on the spot in the line. The end result was that I felt especially blessed not only when it happened but for the rest of the week. I can tell you from experience that I wasn't the only one blessed that day.

When I have the privilege of blessing someone, it carries me throughout the rest of the day full of the joy that the Holy Spirit bestows upon you when you are doing God's will on earth as it is in heaven. I fully believe my 'blessing meter' registers even higher than that of the person I prayed for.

Andrew related to me recently, "Just last week, I called our CPA's office to check on the status of our tax return filing. I mentioned to the young lady on the phone that the CPA and I had grown up together and knew each other well. I said to her, 'Tell Chris that I'm praying for him.' This young lady then said, 'Well keep me in your prayers too.'" Andrew asked her what specifically she wanted him to pray about, and she mentioned a sense of direction and purpose in her life. Andrew seized the initiative and started praying for her right then and there. Andrew told me, "Terry, your faith and witness to me about opportunity to pray for people is what encouraged me to step out in faith and pray specifically for this young lady on the phone. It was an awesome experience."

I was a Vietnam Navy veteran, and in the forty-seven years since my discharge, I have only had three occasions when someone bought my meal at a restaurant in appreciation for my service. All three times were in 2021! The latest was in Terrell, Texas, and I was by myself. I noticed a woman with her ten- or eleven-year-old daughter when they got up to go, and I didn't know it was her who bought my dinner until as she passed by, I heard her explain to her daughter why she was doing it. It made me feel so much better about the direction the youth in this country was heading. You have always heard that it is more blessed to give than receive, well, I am here to tell you that woman and her daughter by far received the greater blessing! I may have gotten a free meal, which I was truly thankful for, but having the honor of getting to bless someone else is immeasurable.

The Holy Spirit has pointed out to me several times that refusing a gift or help from someone is really quite selfish in that you are depriving them of a blessing. We think we are trying to be humble by refusing someone's blessing, but in reality, we are snubbing the Holy Spirit who put it in that person's heart to help out.

Andrew, in reviewing this manuscript for me, thought of an incident very similar to my own experiences: Andrew and his wife, Angela were having breakfast at a restaurant some months back, and he was telling Angela how soul-crushing and heart-breaking some aspects of his job were. As he put it, he was just pouring his heart out to her. Andrew didn't realize it at the time, but a man sitting in the booth next to them was listening to their conversation. Just as they were finishing their meal, he walked past them and said, "I have a Bible verse for you," and then he cited the passage. Andrew surprised by the man, froze for a moment, then whipped his phone out, opened the Bible app, and read the passage out loud in front of him. Andrew returned the man's smile and said, "I receive this Bible passage," then they left the restaurant together. When Andrew and his wife, Angela, got back into their car, they both thought *we won't soon forget that encounter.*

If anything, if you feel you don't deserve the blessing, then by all means pay it forward. I think paying forward is a great way of keeping the blessing going. If you think of the feeding of the 5,000 as a model of the Gospel, in that you take a piece of the bread (the Word) and pass it on, no matter how much you take for yourself, there is always some left over to pass on to others. In that sense, the feeding of the 5,000 has never stopped! There is always some Gospel left over to give away. Like the sign at McDonalds, *Billions and Billions served.*

STEWARDSHIP

Are we good stewards of the resources God has given to us? Isn't it our duty to multiply what God has entrusted to us for His glory in order to build up the kingdom? I consider answered prayer and miracles as resources God has entrusted to us to share with others as wonderful evidence that God is faithful in all that He has promised to do. We are also stewards of the people who are part of our lives, whether stranger or family. To be sure, stewardship of our finances is the primary purpose of the practice of stewardship, but it is so much more.

To be quite honest, I learned very late in life to trust God with my finances. We paid our bills first and gave our leftovers to the church. Tithing just doesn't work that way. Even when I knew better, I persisted to operate my budget with a 'me first' attitude. When God shared His abundance with me, I still didn't get it. I suffered through decades of paycheck-to-paycheck living just to make ends meet. My cars would somehow sense when I was about to go on vacation and break down, and the repairs would cost exactly what I had saved. I joked about leaving the house backward, so our car wouldn't know we were leaving on vacation.

Early proof that God blesses the cheerful giver came when I was working in Seattle at Todd Shipyards, building what was called by the Navy, 'fast frigates.' Do you remember in the Gulf War with Iraq, when the USS Stark (FFG 31) was struck by an Iraqi missile and was nearly destroyed? I worked on that ship for almost eighteen months as a marine sheet metal mechanic between 1981 and 1984. I was intimately familiar with the potential for devastating damage where the missile struck because it was in the forward berthing compartment where a lot of the sailors were quartered.

The shipyards deducted a certain percentage of every paycheck and put it toward our retirement. If you became vested after five years, they would match the money 2 to 1 for your eventual retirement. Well, as it turned out, massive layoffs came after I had been there just three years. I was told upon being laid off; they would return all of my contributions in six months. They even gave me the exact amount I was to receive. I decided to pledge 10 percent to my church when I received the check. I didn't think much about it until the day the check arrived. I soon discovered that the amount I received was exactly 10 percent more than they had quoted me. God proved to me in a mighty way what it meant to have your finances blessed. The donation had literally cost me nothing extra!

But did I learn anything from this? No! I continued giving the way I had always done. I really didn't start tithing until I was almost sixty-five! What a fool I have been for not trusting God sooner. It is the principle of first fruits—you give the first 10 percent before a dime leaves your hand. God will then bless the remainder in ways you cannot imagine. I have had an abundance ever since. It is extraordinary what peace of mind I have experienced.

Shortly after we began tithing, we sold our house and bought an RV trailer and parked it at Sky Point RV Park and Resort on Lake Tawakoni southeast of Dallas. I had a doctor's appointment in Rockwall one afternoon right before Christmas, and we had heard that the Quinlan police had a list of needy people in the community, who needed help. We stopped by the food bank across from the police station long enough to tell the director that when we got back from the doctor's office, we would come back and give something toward helping those people on the list. She said they would be closed by then and to go to Walmart and buy gift cards in $50 increments for the recipients, then bring them by her house, which she pointed out just down the street. We ended up buying $500 worth of cards and went by the director's house as instructed, then went home to do our laundry.

Our RV did not have a washer and dryer so we gathered up the dirty clothes and headed back into Quinlan to a laundry mat. After we put all the clothes in the machines, we noticed that adjoining the laundry mat was a small game room that had miniature slot machines. To kill time until the washing machines were done, I put in about three or four dollars and began to play the minimum bet and almost immediately I hit a jackpot. Since I didn't bet the maximum, it paid out a reduced jackpot—five hundred dollars, the exact same amount that we had decided to give the food bank, and the sun hadn't even set on the same day! I don't want to encourage gambling by any means, but you have to admit the message was obvious. God blesses those who bless others! The truth is that we have really been blessed since we started tithing. Surprisingly, I make more money now in retirement than when I worked full time. If only . . .

Even before I retired, I believed my stewardship duties carried over to the funds I was responsible for at work. Since my position put me over the code enforcement division in Terrell, it was my duty to get high weeds and grass mowed on vacant lots and abandoned houses. Enter Ricky Mendez again, as code enforcement supervisor, he would process complaints, and we would try and get the high weeds and grass mitigated as cheaply as possible since it was on the tax payers dime. We typically sent out a request for sealed bids to have a contractor do the mowing. However, I had the discretion to let someone else do a portion of the work.

Anyone who lived or worked in Terrell knew George Johnson. He drove all around town in a motorized wheelchair. He lived on the south side of town in a poor neighborhood known for its dilapidated houses. He went to church north of the downtown area and would ride his wheelchair there regardless of the weather. His church also operated a large food pantry that was open once a week in which he volunteered every week. He would pull a small lawn mower trailer behind his wheelchair to deliver food to disabled shut-ins. He would also carry their trash out to the curb for them.

Despite his rough and gruff nature, he had a heart of pure gold. One of his church members bought him a riding lawn mower, and he could ride it as well as he could his wheelchair. He agreed to mow vacant lots in his neighborhood and charged well under the going price that contractors charged. So, as it turned out, he not only saved the taxpayers a ton of money, he did a much better job. As long as he could earn a little extra money, he could make ends meet even with his meager disability check.

George told it like he saw it, and he always prefaced his opinion with, "Now, I don't mean no harm." He was a real fixture in the Terrell community until his death in the summer of 2021. I had to stretch the rules considerably to allow him to mow lots for the city, but my view of stewardship includes utilizing human resources, such as George, as well as good financial stewardship.

IT'S A GOD THING

There is just too much evidence for the presence and actions of the Holy Spirit to ignore. We experience events almost daily that the general secular culture tries to suppress and tries to write off supernatural occurrences off as coincidences. I am sure as a believer, you have heard it said, "There is no such thing as a coincidence." Well, I am just going to call these incidents, 'a God thing!' If you try to explain this to a secular audience, they just roll their eyes and you will often catch them winking at each other with that 'knowing' look. They think you're a crazy lunatic and are not really safe around their children. But as we know, this is all foolishness to them, and let's not fall into the trap of trying to fit in with their crowd. I just don't feel the need to explain anything to them. I just say, 'It's a God thing.' My hope is that they will go away thinking that they missed some profound cosmic truth and that will eat away at them until they are prompted to ask for a real explanation which I can take as an invitation to share the Gospel.

The manifestations of the Holy Spirit don't have to be earth shattering events. Many times, the Holy Spirit just shows up unannounced to give us a little reminder He is still there. I think of the time I was traveling to Ft. Worth about sixty miles from my house, and I wasn't having a particularly banner day. I just said a silent prayer, "*God, show me Your presence today.*" I then began to notice almost every car had a Christian bumper sticker all the way to Ft. Worth. The more I looked for them, the more I saw. I have never noticed that many before or since. Needless to say, I forgot what was even bothering me because I was concentrating so much on looking at bumper stickers. This is what I mean by a God thing. In the same manner that I learned to look for the Christian bumper stickers, we need to learn to look for the working of God's presence all around us. The Christian bumper stickers were always there; I just didn't see them until I became sensitive to look for them.

My dad, Don, struggled with diabetes for many years. His diabetes eventually resulted in the amputation of both legs below the knees. After his first amputation, he suffered tremendously from pain, so much so he was taking morphine to combat the pain. He took so much that he was diagnosed with acute morphine poisoning, and the doctor was amazed he was even still alive. That night, he had a vision in his sleep in which a cup was offered to him and he reached out to take the cup, still asleep with his eyes closed. My mother saw him reaching into the air as if to get something but couldn't see anything. The cup was offered to him three times, and each time he would reach for the cup, and when he went to drink from it, he had the sensation of a warm liquid going down that began to go throughout his whole body warming him from head to toe.

The next day the doctors were to begin the tricky business of trying to detoxify his body. When they administered the tests to determine how much morphine he had in his system, they could find no trace of the narcotic. The doctor was so astounded that he wrote a long letter to my dad verifying that according to his professional medical opinion that a bona fide miracle had occurred. I read the letter myself, and I was told that the doctor actually published his findings in a medical journal, but I never saw the article. I guess this definitely qualifies as a God thing!

My wife, Linda, was driving back to Royse City one night from Wylie with her sister, Sharon, and it was so foggy they could barely make out only one white stripe at a time. Traveling on State Highway 205, they were going very slowly and mainly watching the edge of the road to try and stay in their lane. They could not see the turn they had to make on County Road 552, when suddenly a deep voice slowly said, "T-u-u-u-r-n." They went ahead and turned, obeying the voice and ended right in the proper lane on F.M. 552! The oddest thing was that the radio was not even on, so it could not have been the radio! Both heard the voice so it couldn't be written off as a figment of imagination. Both started screaming in complete shock on hearing the voice. Yeah, it was a God thing! Some things sound more like ghost stories. By the way, when Jesus was accused of being a ghost, He never denied the existence of ghosts. That is food for thought and a discussion for another time.

When we lived on Peterson Street in Royse City, we had deep cabinets, and Linda turned the kitchen upside down trying to find a particular pan and had given up when she declared, "Lord, where is that pan?" She asked that in a moment of frustration, more to herself than to God or anything, yet at that moment, the pan came flying out and landed in her lap as she was squatting down in front of the cabinet! The cabinet was too deep for it just to fall out from the back. Ghost story, coincidence, or answered prayer? You decide for yourself; I quit trying to explain 'coincidences' a long time ago. How can the God who manages the entire universe take the time from His infinitely complex schedule to find a lost pan? But doesn't that confirm God loves us enough to answer even trivial requests? I mean if God answers a frustrated call for help finding a lost pan, isn't He capable of answering much more important prayers? Does a prayer request have to rise to the level of a Category 5 hurricane before you bother to pray? Does God only answer desperately important prayers and ignore little prayers? I think this proves God is not some distant deity like so many of the world religions, but a down-to-earth, personal God who loves us beyond our imagination. Metaphor intended.

Could it have been a manifestation of a guardian angel on assignment from God, assigned to be watching over us all the time and waiting for an opportunity to help us at a moment's notice? Did the guardian angel just kick the pan out onto her lap out of boredom because nothing big had happened for a while? I know I'm being facetious, but the reality of an invisible spirit world is something we need to take very seriously. Our faith and belief in prayer being answered is absolutely dependent upon believing that supernatural involvement in our lives is possible albeit unexplainable. As am I writing this, it is the day before Easter, and I am reminded the greatest supernatural event in history occurred, which is the Resurrection of our Lord Jesus Christ! Do I believe that God things happen? They have been happening for thousands of years.

A few years ago, eight of our family members wanted to be baptized, and we arranged to use my stepson's built-in, heated spa tub attached to his swimming pool. It had been raining all day, and I finally said jokingly, "We're going to have a Jericho baptism. We are going to march around the house in the rain seven times until you are all soaking wet, and I'll pronounce you baptized." Fortunately, it stopped raining that afternoon long enough to baptize everyone. It has been such an honor to do this, especially since the requests were unsolicited. When my grandkids asked to be baptized, it was because they had been observing us practicing what we preached, not because of what we had said to them. The day was Sunday, May 24, 2015, the day of Pentecost, the day that celebrates the pouring out of the Holy Spirit! What else but another God thing!

The day was August 24, 2015, and it was late, around 11 p.m. Linda had just arrived from picking up my grandson, Gage, who was staying with us. A blowout on his car had forced him to leave it at a friend's house. Linda had an eye infection, so she went to bed immediately, and I put some eye drops in her eyes that the doctor had prescribed earlier. Even though it was late, I decided to go into our office and read my Bible before going to bed. Gage had been in the kitchen, boiling water for some ramen noodles and had returned to his room to watch television.

My nose started running all of a sudden, so I went into the kitchen to get a napkin that was on the counter next to the stove. When I reached for a napkin, I smelled the strong odor of gas. I checked each knob on the stove and discovered the last one was turned to the lowest setting. The flame had gone out, but the gas wasn't completely turned off. The urge to read my Bible late that night and the fact that my nose suddenly starting running is no doubt that small, still voice saying, "Go to the kitchen." It was actually closer to go to the bathroom for some tissue. I felt such a strong presence of the Holy Spirit, I went and woke Linda up to tell her what just happened. What can I say, guardian angels are a God thing!

Speaking of guardian angels, did you know they even keep you from having to wash dishes? I really don't remember what year it was, maybe between 2002 and 2003, when I was working for the City of Wylie. In the old downtown historic district is a family restaurant called the Ballard Street Café with exposed original brick on the inside and old pictures of Wylie all over the brick walls. It is a real gem, and everyone in Wylie has probably eaten there dozens of times.

It was Saturday and my son Sam had driven about fifty miles to meet me for breakfast. We had just finished eating when the waitress came by and left our ticket on the corner of our table. Even before I could pick it up, the former mayor of Wylie, Don Hughes, came by and grabbed the bill and said, "This is for the catfish filets you gave me." I had given him the fish several months earlier. So, I just replied, "Then I will get the tip."

When I reached for my wallet, I realized that I had left it at home. My son, like most young'uns these days, also didn't have a dime. When we got out to the car, I asked, "Do you realize that a guardian angel just bought our breakfast?" I really didn't feel like washing dishes anyway! God thing? Absolutely!

Right after I got out of the Navy, before I went off to college, I attended my mother's church in Azle. On one particular Sunday, I experienced an incredible vision. A giant, pure-white staircase appeared on the wall behind the pulpit. The height of the stairs was so high it disappeared from view. There was a light emanating from the top, so bright and intense I could not even look at it. In the vision, I began climbing the stairs, and the intense light felt like a strong hot wind that penetrated right through me so that I had to lean into it as I struggled to climb the stairs with my arm shielding my eyes from the brilliant light. I could only imagine that the throne of God was at the top and that the light had to burn away any impurities in my body as well as in my thoughts in order to approach the throne. My view of the whole episode was like watching a movie of me ascending the stairs. In the vision, I never made it all the way to the top before it ended.

My second vision was that of a beautiful scene of rolling hills and meadows with green, knee-high grass swaying in a gentle breeze. There was a crystal-clear river flowing slowly from somewhere in the distance as it meandered through one of the valleys. There was a huge tree in the distance that was located near the bank with large, spreading branches that provided ample shade for what appeared to be a group of people sitting on the ground listening to someone who stood facing them. I had a guide of sorts accompanying me, who answered my questions as we traveled across the meadows. We never came close enough to the people under the tree to hear their voices or identify who they were.

I became curious about whether there were fish in the river. The guide said, "Let's go see." We simply walked into the river where we could see perfectly under the water, and I was pleasantly surprised I didn't have to hold my breath. I saw all kinds of fish of different sizes and colors. When we emerged from the river, I was equally surprised we were not even wet.

I asked the guide what was on a distant hill and he said, "Let's go see." Instantly, we were transported to the hill as if our thoughts transported us there. This is when my vision ended, and I cannot even remember what the hill looked like up close. Both of these visions occurred in the mid-1970s. I have never had another vision, and both of these occurred while I was wide awake. Years later when I took the time to read the entire Bible for the first time, I discovered *Revelation 22:1–2*. I cannot yet ascribe any meaning to the vision or imply what it may mean. I never got a clear understanding of the identity of my guide; however, the scripture below suggests it could have been an angel. I will simply say these visions have helped solidify my faith in much the same way miracles have. Truly, *I have seen too much* to lose my faith now.

> *Then the angel showed me a river of the water of life, clear as crystal, flowing from the throne of God and of the Lamb (Christ), in the middle of its street. On either side of the river was the tree of life, bearing twelve kinds of fruit, yielding its fruit every month; and the leaves of the tree were for the healing of the nations. (Rev. 22:1–2)*

On Monday, December 14, 2015, my mom, Lorraine, had suffered a severe stroke and was in the hospital in downtown Fort Worth. We live about thirty miles east of Dallas just south of Interstate 30, and she was in a hospital also close to I-30 in Fort Worth just over sixty miles away. On Wednesday as we were driving to the hospital, we decided to pull off the freeway in Arlington to get something to eat. We took the exit at Collins Street and headed south past the Dallas Cowboy's stadium. We passed by dozens of restaurants, but nothing appealed to us, so we kept going all the way to Division Street and turned back west, again finding nothing. When we got to Cooper Street, we turned north back toward the freeway again. Just as we got back to the freeway, we spotted a little diner called *Tom's Burgers* on the other side of the street, so we had to cross over the freeway and turn around and come back.

When our food was served, Linda and I joined hands to say grace and said a quick prayer for mom. Just then I heard someone behind me praying out loud, and when I turned around, I found a group of eight men praying together. When they had finished praying, I got up and approached their table and stated I really appreciated that they were not embarrassed to show their faith in public. I mentioned that my mother was in the hospital after suffering from a stroke and asked if they would mind praying for her. The man sitting closest to me at the end of the table said, "Sure, what's her name and yours?" We all joined hands, and they proceeded to pray out loud for my mom.

Of all the restaurants we could have gone to, we arrived at that particular one just as the men began praying out loud! What an incredible display of God's grace. I later realized that the day she had the stroke was my mom and dad's anniversary. It was in that moment that I knew God was calling her home as my dad had already gone ahead of her.

I printed out the words to Bing Crosby's song, "I'll Be Home for Christmas" and pinned it to the wall of her hospital room and had everyone write notes on it. My mom passed away on Sunday, December 20. On Monday, my brother, Russell and his wife Mary, my sister Marlene, my aunt Dorothy, and I had to go to the funeral home to sign all the papers and make arrangements for the service. We got finished about 1 p.m., so we decided to go to a nearby Mexican restaurant in Lake Worth. As we were eating our lunch the song, *"I'll Be Home for Christmas"* began playing on the restaurant's sound system.

Afterward, we all gathered at my sister's house to look at old family photos of mom and the family. My son, Sam, was digging through one of the boxes and found a poem my aunt Dorothy had written for my mom several months earlier entitled, "I'm Free." We all agreed that it should be read at the funeral service. The following Monday, we had to go back to the funeral home to make final arrangements. Marlene and I were taken back to small office where we were asked to pick out the service bulletin pattern from a large binder. The very first sample was entitled, "I'm Free"! Coincidence? I think *not*! But this isn't the end of the story.

My brother, Troy, died in 1990 on my mom's birthday, June 3rd. Russell told me at mom's funeral something I had never heard before. When my brother Troy had died, my mother had his remains cremated. We took his ashes out to Lake Worth to spread his ashes in the lake. There were seven kids (1 girl and 6 boys) in our family, and we all grew up at our lake house right on Lake Worth across from Carswell Air Force Base in the 1960s. For us, it was a virtual paradise for kids, swimming and fishing every day of the summer vacation. So, it was really appropriate to spread Troy's ashes there. I had a large deck boat that could accommodate a lot of people, which was perfect for our task at hand.

When my dad put the first scoop of Troy's ashes into the water, a vision of Troy suddenly appeared coming out of the water exclaiming, "*I'm Free!*" My dad bolted upright on his seat startled by the vision, and my mom started to sing a hymn. My mom and dad were the only ones who saw or heard the vision and didn't even tell each other what they saw for almost a year.

At my mom's service I shared this wonderful display of God's grace with the audience. My mom was a true prayer warrior. At her service, I told the gathering of family and friends that if my mom knew your name, then you *had* been prayed for!

A couple a days later, Linda and I were headed to a movie theater in Mesquite and stopped by a *Red Lobster* restaurant to get a gift card for my mom's pastor who conducted the service. As I entered the restaurant, my phone's alert system went off warning us to take cover because a tornado was headed right for us. We decided to go home instead of going to the movies. Stopping to get the gift card at Red Lobster delayed us just long enough to get the warning in time to make it back across the Lake Ray Hubbard bridge heading into Rockwall. We had barely crossed the bridge when the tornado struck, destroying whole apartment complexes along with dozens of homes adjacent to the bridge. It even caught four vehicles on the approach to the bridge where we had been moments before and tossed them over the guardrail to the street forty feet below. The first thing I intend to do when I get to heaven is to find my guardian angels and give them one gigantic hug!

When you experience a close call like that and you know but by the grace of God you were spared you can't help but believe in real Guardian Angels—you *know* it is a God thing!

Andrew routinely and regularly tells people who have been in accidents and escaped death "If you've ever wondered if God the Father has a purpose for your life, you have your answer. God does have a purpose and calling on your life, or you would not be here."

I had never been up to New England before to visit my brothers until 2018. My brothers, Keith, Monte, and Russell moved up to the Boston area in the eighties as part of a massive cleanup of Boston Harbor that was on EPA's Superfund environmental hazard list. My brother, Monte, led a pretty wild life most of his life, but when I visited him in 2018, he had slowed down considerably as cancer and alcohol began to take their toll. In a moment of severe abdominal pain, Monte went out to his car and sat in the driver's seat because he could tolerate the pain much better there. Russell soon joined us, and the mood was rather somber as the realization that Monte was dying sank in. I said it was about time they both got right with God, and they both nodded in agreement. I led them in a quick prayer of repentance, and they both invited Jesus into their hearts. It was very reminiscent of the thief on the cross in that Monte would soon be home with the Savior in Paradise. It was a sad occasion for me because I knew Monte didn't have time to enjoy serving Christ as I have had the privilege of doing most of my life. I had the satisfaction of knowing he would be waiting on the other side for me. It would be the last time I ever got to see him alive. Soon, I had to return to Texas, and I never got to attend his funeral.

Another instance of God's mercy and grace came at the deathbed of my wife's ex-husband, Freddy, when I actually got to lead him to Christ. I would run into Freddy at most of the birthday parties for the kids, grandkids, or great-grandkids. If you know your math, that adds up to nearly forty birthdays a year! When Freddy entered the hospital, the prognosis was not very optimistic about winning his battle with bone cancer. Linda and I went to the hospital mostly to show our support for the kids. So, I did not go with any expectation of getting to witness to him. It just happened in the course of our visit.

Freddy had remarried well over twenty years earlier even before Linda and I married in 1999. At the hospital, I asked Freddy and his family including his wife, Karen, if I could have a moment alone with him, and they nodded their assent. I asked Freddy if he knew what I was going to ask him, and he nodded again. I proceeded to lead him in the sinner's prayer, and he genuinely asked God to forgive him and come into his heart. When the word came to his children, Dwayne, Glenn, and Shelly, that he had dedicated his life to Jesus before he died, which happened very quickly after our visit, it had a profound effect on them. It was one of those moments when God chose to use me as His vessel of grace.

It is an overwhelming thought of what the implications would be if I had given an excuse to God that it was none of my business or such as that. It is like the watchman on the wall who does not give warning; then the blood is on his head. I hope I never have to stand before God and have to account for somebody's absence from heaven. God things will happen a lot more often if we just open our hearts in obedience. I continue to be profoundly grateful to God that in His infinite mercy that He allows us to come to the cross like the thief in the last moments of our life.

BOUNDARIES

I can't talk about these miracles and not leave you any tools to use in spreading the Good News. I have already stated that when we experience a miracle or answered prayer or any of the hundreds, if not thousands or millions of ways God reveals himself to us, we are obligated to tell others. Think of people you don't know as brothers and sisters in Christ you just haven't met yet. So, I asked the question. "How can you go about spreading the Gospel in a meaningful way and overcome our natural fear of talking to strangers or shyness when we are trying to get up enough courage to say something?" This first tool is called *Boundaries* and is for personal interaction with others, such as family, friends, coworkers, and people at church—in other words, those people we know so we can practice our faith on familiar faces. The next step is to try it with people you run into as we go about our everyday business: the waiter at the restaurant, nurses at the doctor's office, your child's teacher, the daycare, or the park, and so forth. You get the idea. Andrew and I pray that God will send someone into our path, who needs encouragement, prayer, or the Gospel. If you ask, God will send people into your path. You can't imagine the joy you will experience if you reach out to be a blessing to others. Believe me, you will be more blessed than the person you impart the blessing to. Both Andrew and I can vouch for that.

The second tool is the 'Barefoot Brigade.' This doesn't have to have personal interaction. In fact, it can be done entirely alone or in any size group. It is about spiritual warfare and is something even the shyest person can participate in. No training is necessary, and the only requirement is a sincere heart for prayer. It is very satisfying to your soul when you are engaging the enemy and taking back territory for the kingdom. Start with your home first, just take your shoes off and declare your home as holy to the Lord and sanctify it by dedicating it to God. Then start visiting around your neighborhood and expand your horizons.

You should guess by now I have a real gift for gab. I have been accused all my life of talking too much. Guilty as charged. Once when I was in the Navy, my division officer LTJG Bonner put on my evaluation, "Terry has an excellent command of the English language." My only regret is that I haven't had the discipline to talk to God as much as I talk to everyone else. I have learned to take full advantage of my 'gift of gab,' however, in that I have absolutely no qualms about striking up a conversation even with perfect strangers. I have always enjoyed joking around with people in line at the grocery store, the waiting room at the doctor's office, or anywhere for that matter. Whenever the time seems right, I open the conversation with a little humor. Humor has always been my strong suit, and it is easy to segue into discussions about faith after breaking the ice with a little levity.

Andrew's dad did the very same thing when he was in the hospital paralyzed for four months. He shared the love of God and salvation through Jesus to everyone. Andrew said, "When I was with Dad visiting, we would sing the old hymn songs out of the church hymnal and anytime anyone entered the room, I would invite them to sing along. Everyone demurred and said they couldn't sing." Andrew's response was, "God said to make a joyful noise and this is 'the singing room' here in the hospital." They would all laugh and believe it or not, about half of the people would join in and sing along, recalls Andrew.

This illustration that I call Boundaries is the easiest way to share the Gospel I have ever found. You have just got to try it. It is so much fun to see the "Aha" moment come into someone's face as they recognize the final reveal. Several years ago, I was reading Jonathan Cahn's book, *The Book of Mysteries,* and nearing the end of the book, I came across a particular mystery called, "*The Four Corners of the Altar*" on Day number 332 in his book. Although, the *mystery* never mentions boundaries and what they represent, the principle, however, used in my illustration is similar, and I was inspired to share the Gospel utilizing a drawing of a rectangular figure I call Boundaries.

I simply print the rectangular pattern with my computer and cut them out. I pre-fold them with a sharp crease in the right places and carry them in my wallet so when the opportunity to share the Gospel through this illustration arises, I am ready. I have used napkins at restaurants, a page torn from a notebook, or just about any available blank piece of paper to show the demonstration. The typical reaction of the viewer is one of complete surprise when the final shape is revealed. I get a knowing look when the shape is ultimately recognized and a satisfying expression of "A-A-H-H-H!" slips from their lips.

When I showed it to our landlady and her husband at the RV Park where we were staying at the time, her reaction was that it gave her goose bumps.

When I had my first stroke in November 2019, I shared it with the nurses, doctors, radiology staff, and even the hospital chaplain. The illustration opened all kinds of conversations, allowing me to further explore the Gospel with them. During my second stint at the hospital with my second stroke, I was able to share it with many more of the hospital staff, including my physical and occupational therapists. The staff started coming by my room in order for me to pray for their family members and for other requests. One of the occupational therapists named Cici said, "I don't want you to take this the wrong way, but I believe God sent you to this hospital just for me." She has an autistic son who has left her spiritually and physically drained. We prayed for her son every chance we got. This door was opened when I shared the Boundaries illustration with her.

One morning at our normal prayer time, around 8 a.m., I called Andrew and asked him to call me back at precisely 9:05 a.m. At 9:00 a.m. sharp, in walked Nikki, one of my occupational therapists for the morning's rehab activities. After I had shared the Boundaries illustration with her several days earlier, she began to tell me how she and her husband of only six months studied their Bibles together every chance they got. Every time she was scheduled to help me with my rehab, she would invariably want to talk about the scriptures they had read the night before. Nikki reminded me of the conversations I have with my daughter, Anna, as we discuss biblical truths.

The phone rang right on cue at 9:06, and much to her surprise, when I put the call on speaker, Andrew said, "Nikki, Terry has told me so much about how you and your husband study the Bible together. I am calling so that Terry and I can pray and ask God to bless your marriage." The overwhelming emotions she felt was clearly visible as tears of joy ran down her face.

As a side note, every nurse, regardless of the purpose of their visit is required to ask me what my birthday is for verification purposes. When Nikki first heard when my birthday was, she exclaimed, "That's my birthday too!"

I can say unequivocally that every nurse I encountered during my one-month stay at Presbyterian Hospital in Dallas was a devout Christian and were always encouraging me as they went about their daily duties. I am positive that the degree to which I rapidly recovered from my stroke was directly related to all the prayers that were sent on my behalf from my family and friends and the entire nursing staff at the hospital. I have to give a special shout out to my physical therapist, Neil, who day in and day out had such a contagious cheerful disposition that I looked forward to the daily torture – just kidding, Neil. The saying I heard recently really does describe the hospital staff I encountered, "If you save one life you are a hero, if you save a hundred lives you are a nurse." Every time my doctors made their rounds, they were noticeably impressed by the progress I made just from the previous visit.

You start out simply by asking the question, "Can I show you something?" You start by showing them the rectangle and explain, "This rectangle represents the boundaries in your life. Some are self-imposed, some are imposed by the government, your employer, or your family. Some are the result of our culture, moral standards, your age, your health, your faith, your education, experience, or your job. You will live your entire life constrained by these boundaries."

After the above explanation, you deliver the punch line, "The question is, how do you think outside the box?" You then take the rectangle (you should pre-fold it and crease it so it is easy to tear apart) and tear it in half length ways down the middle. Then tear it in half crossways about a third of the way down from one end. Reassemble the rectangle on a table or other convenient flat surface. (see illustrations) Then repeat the question, "So, how do you think outside the box?" Take each corner and turn it in place 180 degrees, aligning it back close to each other piece. The box then forms a perfect cross in the middle and you triumphantly declare, "With Christ at the center of your life you now have no boundaries!"

The door is now wide open to discuss the Gospel in depth or if they do not have time to discuss things further, such as the waitress I mentioned earlier, then I just hand them the torn-up rectangle for a keepsake. A very fertile seed has been planted.

When all you have to do is open your heart and let Jesus come in, what is the consequence of rejecting Jesus? This poem I wrote on the back of my church bulletin on Mother's Day, May 8, 2016 says it all:

Unclaimed Mail

Sins forgiven by God but His grace was never claimed,
How many mansions in heaven will be vacant?
How many people could have been there?
Rejecting the gift of salvation when it came to them.
"Return to Sender," they said.
Jesus had no choice but to stamp "Undeliverable" on their hearts!

The Church is called the bride of Christ. Salvation through Jesus Christ is much like a marriage proposal. Jesus proposes to each person and asks them to marry Him. We have the choice to answer 'yes' or 'no.' When we accept Jesus as our personal Lord and Savior, He comes into our lives and exchange takes place. Jesus takes our place on the cross, pays our debt to God for sin, and in exchange, Jesus gives us His righteousness, His justification, and His sanctification.

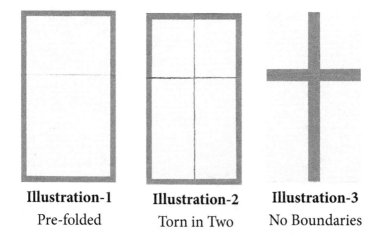

Illustration-1   **Illustration-2**   **Illustration-3**
Pre-folded   Torn in Two   No Boundaries

THE BAREFOOT BRIGADE

O n September 22, 2014, I was listening to a talk show host on American Family Radio, and he closed the show with the words, "May God bless your socks off!" I don't remember who said this, but it inspired me to create the Barefoot Brigade. The idea is to sanctify places to the Lord as 'Holy Ground.' We all know that Satan has carved this world into spiritually depraved strongholds (Eph. *6:12*). God only knows how our institutions and especially our schools have become spiritual battlegrounds. Well, it's about time we take them back. It's time to take our faith on the road and start taking the fight to the enemy. I had been looking for easy practical ways to demonstrate our faith and to bear fruit for the kingdom. This is a simple task, fun to do and is especially great fun for children to participate in.

The Barefoot Brigade is simply a call for all Christians to put on the 'full armor of God' and consecrate churches, schools, court houses, government offices (city, state and federal), work places, homes, and so forth to God and declare the grounds as holy to the Lord and that the Word of God and truth would be proclaimed and abided by in every place and in every activity. You simply take your shoes off and sanctify the location, facility, and/or activities by declaring the property as being holy to the Lord.

When the new high school/ junior high was being built in the Tidehaven School District, Andrew and his two boys, Adam and Nathan, consecrated the building as it was being built. Andrew noticed as the steel beams and columns were going up, that the iron workers used large yellow crayons to mark on the steel columns. This gave him an idea. Andrew asked the steel foreman if he could have three of those yellow crayons and explained to him what he wanted to do. When Andrew finished explaining his intentions, the foreman smiled really big and handed Andrew three large yellow crayons. Adam, Nathan, and Andrew took those large yellow crayons and wrote Bible verses on every single vertical column in the building. Then when they finished that, we went back over every column with *another* Bible verse, then again, a third time. They particularly concentrated on the staircase in the library where Angela was going to be working, and they wrote Bible verses on every single step that spoke of God ordering the steps of a righteous man or following in the steps of Christ, and so on. Andrew recalls that was a very big moment for him and the boys.

Additionally, Andrew dedicated the cornerstones of three campuses while they were under construction. He wrote out this Bible verse on the back of each cornerstone in black permanent marker: "Suffer the little children to come unto me for such is the Kingdom of Heaven." And then he signed his name and dated each one.

Similarly, when our new house was being built in Royse City, Linda and I took some of our grandkids over to the construction site after the framing was done and had them write their names on the backing of the fireplace while we wrote Bible verses on the door headers and transoms. When we finally moved in, we felt so much better about the house since we had sanctified it.

Understand that putting on the full armor of God isn't just a defensive posture that we assume to protect ourselves and our families from the enemy, although that certainly is one of the primary reasons we put on the armor. But why do we prepare for battle with no intention of joining the battle? Jesus did not intend for us to be pacifists when it comes to spiritual warfare. The Barefoot Brigade is just such an opportunity to suit up and go attack the enemy on his own turf, his strongholds as it were. Why wait until the enemy attacks you first? Gather your troops and lead them into battle! Remember we have already won through Christ, and "Bub" is already defeated. We are just in a cleanup role, putting out hotspots left over from the main battle.

We all know very little truth is being presented in our schools, media, and especially in our government by politicians. I am also sure that you are aware that a spiritual blindness has descended upon this great country of ours, and our religious freedom is under attack in every quarter. It is time we took America back one place at a time. The Barefoot Brigade is not a nonprofit organization; there is no website or phone numbers to call or formal leadership that can be attacked or ridiculed by the cancel culture on social media and therefore isn't subject to the wokeness mongers. The IRS cannot audit it; the Supreme Court cannot pass judgments against it because the Barefoot Brigade is simply people declaring the truth.

Go to your local schools, city hall, and other institutions and declare the ground as holy to God. If you see a place of ungodly activity, such as an abortion clinic or an atheist organization, declare their property as holy to the Lord. Then, just for fun, send them an anonymous letter proclaiming that their property has been dedicated to God and sign it, 'The Barefoot Brigade,' which will drive them crazy! Anyone can join and become a member of the Brigade. The only qualification is that you have been commissioned by Jesus to spread the Good News. My wife and I took a picture of us standing barefooted on the State Seal of Texas in the capitol rotunda in Austin, Texas, when we consecrated our state capitol to God.

So, take your shoes off and lift up the places in your community and dedicate them to God—let's take back our country in Jesus's name!

Consecrate a fast, call a sacred assembly; Gather the elders and all the inhabitants of the land Into the house of the Lord your God, and cry out to the Lord.

(Joel 1:14)

"Then He said, "Do not draw near this place. Take your sandals off your feet, for the place where you stand is holy ground.

(Exod. 3:5)

BLESSINGS

*All these are the twelve tribes of Israel, and this is what their father said to them when he blessed them. He blessed them, every one with the blessing **appropriate** to him. **(Gen. 49:28)***

E ven though this chapter doesn't relate directly to the subject of miracles, I wanted to include it as a way to draw your family even closer together in the Lord. Just think of it as a fun way to start your journey to lead your family toward the Promised Land. The blessings below, that I said over all of our children, are just examples of what the general form could be. Explore the Bible yourself and find those verses that are *appropriate* to your own children. When you do, it will become very personal, and your children will be truly blessed.

After I had the stroke in November 2019, I was keenly aware that my life was but a mere blip in the course of human events. I felt especially aware of the writings of Solomon in *Ecclesiastes* when he came to realize time stops for no one. I felt stuck in the middle of the river of life with its waters swirling around me as it went flooding past me in its relentless journey towards eternity. After having several brushes with death, I was by no means worried I was going to die or even afraid of dying, especially, since I knew I was on borrowed time since nearly drowning in March 2005. As I began to recover from my first stroke, the Holy Spirit asked me. "Why haven't you blessed your children?" I thought about that awhile and wondered just how I was supposed to do that.

Then in February 2021, I received the inspiration from the Holy Spirit that it would be really special if I blessed each of my children like Jacob did in Genesis 49. I toyed with the idea for months with no idea of how to pull it off. Then one day in late November, I sat down at the computer, and it was like taking dictation, much as it has been for this book. As fast as I could type, the words just appeared. I look at the results now, and I can hardly believe they are my words; in fact, now I know that the Holy Spirit was responsible. I am including them here only because I believe every father should take the time to bless his children with an inspirational message to guide them as God, the Father, has done for me and cast a blessing on them as a prophecy that they can confidently grow into the image of God that they are.

It was so much fun to do. I picked a fancy medieval type font and printed them on resume-grade card stock and framed the blessings and attached the associated Bible verses on the back for easy reference. Just like the scripture from Genesis 49 above, I found amazing Bible verses appropriate to each of them. How their personalities and character emerged from the blessings astounded me. It was as if the Bible verses had been written just for them.

I didn't want the framed blessings to be considered just another Christmas present even though I presented them just before Christmas. I gave each blessing to them individually, laid my hands on them, and anointed them with oil after reading the scriptures and the blessing. I wasn't prepared for the profound effect it had on each one of our children.

When I married Linda over twenty years ago, she had three children, Dwayne, Glenn, and Shelly; and I had three children, Chari, Anna, and Sam. She has two older sons and her youngest is her daughter. I, on the other hand, have two older daughters, and my youngest is my son.

It is always a struggle for a parent in a blended family to really gain the full trust and love of their stepchildren. A multitude of natural barriers occur that it sometimes seems you will never reach this lofty plateau. But it is s-o-o-o worthwhile. Both Linda's children and mine are really special as you will be able to discern for yourselves when you read their blessings. There are no signs of jealousy, envy, selfishness, or any hurtful way in them at all; instead you find in them the litany of the fruits of the Spirit:

> *But the fruit of the Spirit is love, joy, peace, patience, kindness, goodness, faithfulness, gentleness, self-control; against such things there is no law.* **(Gal. 5:22–23)**

Both Linda and I received a tremendous blessing from this exercise as well. It has truly brought us together as a blended family. That blending has become like mixing two colors of paint together. We literally cannot be separated again. I hope this book as inspired you to excel still more.

> *Finally, brethren, whatever is true, whatever is honorable, whatever is right, whatever is pure, whatever is lovely, what-ever is of good repute, if there is any excellence and if anything, worthy of praise, dwell on these things.* **(Phil. 4:8)**

Charito Marie George

My daughter Chari, full of grace and wisdom beyond your years, how I have always admired your motherly instincts and dedication to family. The sacrifices you have made on behalf of your family have not been overlooked by God, and your portion in heaven shall be great. Your always-calm and gracious manner in every situation bespeaks of your character and maturity. My prayer for you is that God's plans for you will be accomplished and fulfilled exceedingly beyond all that you can ask or think (Eph. 3:14–21).

I hereby bless you in accordance with the great biblical tradition of the laying on of my hands and anointing you with oil that you may enjoy the fullness of God's grace and love. One of the greatest gifts is our adoption as children of God, and there is nothing stronger than the bond of love between a father and his daughter as you have been the joy of my life (Ps. 25 4–5; Rom. 8:15)!

For this reason I bend my knees before the Father, from whom every family in heaven and on earth derives its name, that He would grant you, according to the riches of His glory, to be strengthened with power through His Spirit in the inner self, so that Christ may dwell in your hearts through faith; and that you, being rooted and grounded in love, may be able to comprehend with all the saints what is the width and length and height and depth, and to know the love of Christ which surpasses knowledge, that you may be filled to all the fullness of God. Now to Him who is able to do far more abundantly beyond all that we ask or think, according to the power that works within us, to Him be the glory in the church and in Christ Jesus to all generations forever and ever. Amen. **(Eph. 3:14–21)**

Make me know Thy ways, O Lord; teach me Thy paths. Lead me in Thy truth and teach me, for Thou art the God of my salvation; for Thee I wait all the day. **(Ps. 25:4–5)**

For you have not received a spirit of slavery leading to fear again, but you have received a spirit of adoption as sons by which we cry out, "Abba Father"! **(Rom. 8:15)**

Freddy Dwayne Hill

I will always consider you to be my son, through the bond of love that only a proud father can feel. You have only shown me respect, which means more to me than you will ever know. Your quiet and easy-going demeanor is a very admirable trait that speaks of your confidence, maturity, and sincerity. Your steadfastness and purpose-driven life invokes my remembrance of a Bible verse I have underlined (Phil. 1:3–6): 'He who began a good work in you will perfect it until the day of Christ Jesus." In the tradition of Jacob in the Bible, I want to give you my blessing and may you love Jesus and believe in Him as I have done (Matt. 5:5–6).

Receive this my blessing at the laying on of my hands and anointing you that the Holy Spirit "may grant you your heart's desire, and fulfill all your purpose" (Ps. 20:4).

I thank my God in all my remembrance of you, always offering prayer with joy in my every prayer for you all, in view of your participation in the gospel from the first day until now. For I am confident of this very thing, that He who began a good work among you will complete it by the day of Christ Jesus. (Phil. 1:3–6)

Blessed are the gentle, for they will inherit the earth. Blessed are those who hunger and thirst for righteousness, for they will be satisfied. **(Matt. 5:5–6)**

May He grant you your heart's desire and fulfill your whole plan! **(Ps. 20:4)**

Anna Lisa Fields

A nna, my daughter, your thirst and hunger for truth in the Word of God will always lead you toward the path of righteousness that will bring you ever closer to our Lord and Savior, Yeshua Hamashiach! It never ceases to amaze me of your knowledge of the Bible and how much you have taught me. The greatest compliment I have ever received in my life is when you asked me to pass on my Bible to you. My fervent prayer and hope is that your love for God's Word will endure and prepare you for what great tasks God has destined you for (Prov. 27:17; Deut. 6:4–9).

I now give you my blessing in accordance with the ancient biblical tradition of anointing you with oil and the laying on of my hands, declaring that the Holy Spirit will continue to dwell mightily in you (Ps. 71:17–18; 119:10–16).

As iron sharpens iron, so one person sharpens another.
(Prov. 27:17)

Hear, O Israel: The Lord our God, the Lord is one! You shall love the Lord your God with all your heart, with all your soul, and with all your strength. And these words which I command you today shall be in your heart. You shall teach them dili-gently to your children, and shall talk of them when you sit in your house, when you walk by the way, when you lie down, and when you rise up. You shall bind them as a sign on your hand, and they shall be as frontlets between your eyes. You shall write them on the doorposts of your house and on your gates. **(Deut. 6:4–9)**

God, You have taught me from my youth,

and I still declare Your wondrous deeds. And even when I am old and gray, God, do not abandon me, until I declare Your strength to this generation, Your power to all who are to come. **(Ps. 71:17–18)**

With my whole heart I have sought You; Oh, let me not wander from Your commandments! Your word I have hidden in my heart, that I might not sin against You. Blessed are You, O LORD! *Teach me Your statutes. With my lips I have declared all the judgments of Your mouth. I have rejoiced in the way of Your testimonies, as much as in all riches. I will meditate on Your precepts, and contemplate Your ways. I will delight myself in Your statutes; I will not forget Your word.* **(Ps. 119:10–16)**

Clifton Glenn Hill

I have always felt as if you were one of my own sons, not through blood, but in the spirit of respect and love. With the greatest of affection and pride, I admire your strength of character and integrity as of a father and his son. The loving kindness you have shown me over the length of our relationship has always warmed my heart and brought us closer together in so many ways (Ps. 1:1–3).

Your love of God, family, and country shines forth like a beacon of light to everyone you meet. You are always ready to defend your faith, family, and friends like a charging lion without hesitation. A quiet strength emanates from your innermost being that imparts confidence and trust in others. Now with the laying on of my hands, I now bless you in the long-standing tradition of the biblical fathers and sons (Eph. 6:11–17; Prov. 3:1–6).

Blessed is the person who does not walk in the counsel of the wicked, nor stand in the path of sinners, nor sit in the seat of scoffers! But his delight is in the Law of the Lord, And on His Law he meditates day and night. He will be like a tree planted by streams of water, which yields its fruit in its season, and

its leaf does not wither; And in whatever he does, he prospers.
(Ps. 3:1–3)

Put on the full armor of God, so that you will be able to stand
firm against the schemes of the devil. For our struggle is not
against flesh and blood, but against the rulers, against the
powers, against the world forces of this darkness, against the
spiritual forces of wickedness in the heavenly places. Therefore,
take up the full armor of God, so that you will be able to resist
on the evil day, and having done everything, to stand firm.
Stand firm therefore, having belted your waist with truth, and
having put on the breastplate of righteousness, and having
strapped on your feet the preparation of the gospel of peace; in
addition to all, taking up the shield of faith with which you will
be able to extinguish all the flaming arrows of the evil one. And
take the helmet of salvation and the sword of the Spirit, which
is the word of God. (Eph. 6:11–17)

My son, do not forget my teaching, but have your heart comply
with my commandments;

For length of days and years of life and peace they will add
to you. Do not let kindness and truth leave you; Bind them
around your neck, Write them on the tablet of your heart. So,
you will find favor and a good reputation in the sight of God
and man. Trust in the Lord with all your heart and do not
lean on your own understanding. In all your ways acknowl-
edge Him, And He will make your paths straight. (Prov. 3:1–6)

Shelly Dawn Hill

My daughter, Shelly, your pure heart of gold and exuberant joy fills every room you enter with love and happiness beyond measure! It is with the greatest affection and pride that I have the honor of calling you my daughter. My hope and constant prayer for you is that God will grant you His grace and loving kindness to match your boundless joy (Prov. 31:29; Ps. 89:15).

In the ancient biblical tradition of blessing one's children, I am laying on my hands and passing on the blessings of God that you may fully enjoy the richness of God's joy and love. The greatest joy I could ever hope for is for my children to come to love and honor our Father who art in heaven, such as I have hopefully done. My love as a father for you, my daughter, is the most precious joy of my life (Ps. 126:2–3)!

Many daughters have done nobly, but you excel them all. (**Prov. 31:29**

Blessed are the people who know the joyful sound! Lord, they walk in the light of Your face. (**Ps. 89:15**)

Then our mouth was filled with laughter and our tongue with joyful shouting; Then they said among the nations, 'The Lord has done great things for them,' The Lord has done great things for us; We are joyful. **(Ps. 126:2)**

SAMUEL CLINTON CAPEHART

I named you Samuel, which means "Gift from God." You are my youngest, but it is God's plan and desire to take the least and use them for the greatest purposes. It was Samuel, the prophet, who anointed David, the youngest son of Jesse, to be the greatest king and the one from whom the Messiah would come (1 Sam. 16:7).

Those who, through sorrows, disappointments, broken dreams, broken hearts, frustration, pain, and tears, are being prepared for great and mighty things. Above all else, may you love Jesus and believe in Him as I have done (Jer. 29:11–13).

Sam, my only son, you have the heart and compassion of the Spirit of God that will always keep you close to God. Receive this my blessing at the laying on of my hands and anointing you that the Holy Spirit may come mightily upon you that you may serve the Lord with all your heart, mind, and body (Rom. 8:28–31; 2 Pet. 1: 5–10).

> *But the Lord said to Samuel, "Do not look at his appearance or at the height of his stature, because I have rejected him; for God does not see as man sees, since man looks at the outward appearance, but the Lord looks at the heart.* **(1 Sam. 16:7)**

For I know the plans that I have for you,' declares the Lord, 'plans for prosperity and not for disaster, to give you a future and a hope. Then you will call upon Me and come and pray to Me, and I will listen to you. And you will seek Me and find Me when you search for Me with all your heart. **(Jer. 29:11–13)**

And we know that God causes all things to work together for good to those who love God, to those who are called according to His purpose. For those whom He foreknew, He also predestined to become conformed to the image of His Son, so that He would be the firstborn among many brothers and sisters; and these whom He predestined, He also called; and these whom He called, He also justified; and these whom He justified, He also glorified. What then shall we say to these things? If God is for us, who is against us? **(Rom. 8:28–31)**

Now for this very reason also, applying all diligence, in your faith supply moral excellence, and in your moral excellence, knowledge, and in your knowledge, self-control, and in your self-control, perseverance, and in your perseverance, godliness, and in your godliness, brotherly kindness, and in your brotherly kindness, love. For if these qualities are yours and are increasing, they do not make you useless nor unproductive in the true knowledge of our Lord Jesus Christ. For the one who lacks these qualities is blind or short-sighted, having forgotten his purification from his former sins. Therefore, brothers and sisters, be all the more diligent to make certain about His calling and choice of you; for as long as you practice these things, you will never stumble. **(2 Pet. 1:5–10)**

My closing prayer, "Dear heavenly Father, use this book inspired by Your Holy Spirit to inspire others. Open their hearts to the truth and Your Word, which is truth. I ask You specifically to bless all those who are striving to serve You and shield them on a daily basis with the wings of your angels. Lift them up on wings like eagles and help them soar on behalf of Your kingdom. I thank you for Your answered prayers and Your grace so generously bestowed upon us. Thank you for Your forgiveness, and teach us to forgive others. Encourage us to reach out to the ones who are perishing and use our hands in prayer to pull them out of the pit and the clutches of the enemy. Finally, confound the enemy in his every effort to destroy us. Remove the teeth from the roaring lion on our behalf and thwart his every plan to devour us. All these things I pray in the precious name of Jesus. Amen and Amen."

HAVE YOU TAKEN
YOUR DAILY VITAMIN 'M'?

U ntil now the stories have been about '*Sure Nuff*' miracles, but what I want to discuss now is the everyday evidence of God's presence all around us. As I shared earlier, I have recovered from cancer twice, suffered two strokes, and nearly drowned. Every day I wake up, it is a miracle to me, and I am thankful to be alive. Like the old limerick, "I wake up in the morning and I shake off my wits. I open the newspaper and read the obits. When my name is not there and I know I'm not dead then I eat a big breakfast and go back to bed!"

If you don't make a conscious effort to recognize that the hand of God is in everything around us, you will miss most of it. Life will just pass us by while we are too busy to stop and smell the roses. So many of us have blinked, and our lives suddenly vanished in the sands of time. Yes, life rolls passed us so fast, and we are totally unprepared for the speed in which it evaporates into the vapor of eternity. At seventy years old, I have so many regrets about letting time slip through my fingers. This chapter is intended to put me in its crosshairs as much as anyone else. If only I had _____ , you fill in the blank. I think it is really impossible not to squander our time; such is life. I mean we all have jobs and a million things that need to be done. The yard needs to be mowed, the dishes need to be washed, and so does the laundry. When was the last time you spent some quality time with your washing machine?

Everyone wants to spend *quality* time with their families. But what does quality time really mean? Living in a materialistic culture, we often equate the word *quality* with wealth and lots of possessions or spending our time on lavish vacations. It is easy to get caught up in the rat race of keeping up with the Jones. Solomon, who was the wealthiest man who ever lived, realized that it didn't buy him happiness. Is wealth and possessions, then, a bad thing? Of course not. But everything has to be put in perspective. What is that perspective you ask? Throughout our lives, things happen that force us or gives us the opportunity to 'put things into perspective.' Andrew's dad once told him that when his mom nearly died from colon cancer and how she flatlined twice in the hospital, his whole perspective changed. How he offered God everything he owned, the house, the land, the cattle, everything, if only He would allow his wife to live. She did live. Andrew's dad's life was changed dramatically from the point. It was a story Andrew's dad shared many times over the years.

The realization that we are created in the image of God is a good beginning. What that means is that every human being who has ever lived on earth was created with a void in their hearts and lives. It is a God-shaped void that can only be filled by God. Things get out of kilter when we try to fill that void with anything else—work, money, possessions, alcohol, drugs, sex, or any number of the thousands of things that mankind uses to try to fill that void with. We have all suffered emptiness and loneliness because we don't have the proper perspective. Our whole world and everything in it belong to God, and He loves us so much; it was all made just for us to enjoy.

Remember, how in Genesis, God used to enjoy walking through the Garden of Eden in the cool of the evening just to have a pleasant conversation with Adam and Eve. I really believe if we hand over our lives, jobs, finances, possessions, families, health, and especially our worries to God and let Him become the center of our lives, we can once again enjoy fellowship with Him in the cool of the evening. Look around you, what have you got to lose? Life is precious, and it really can only be enjoyed with Jesus at the center of our lives.

I know many of you are afraid if you let go you will lose control of your life and you may not like where you land. Isn't it about whether you trust God or not? Whether you will like where He takes you? In the case of many of the famous so-called 'New Atheists' like Christopher Hitchens, Richard Dawkins, Stephen Hawking, Carl Sagan, and the like, "It's not like I don't believe in God; I just don't want there to be a God telling me what to do," as Christopher Hitchens famously said before he died. Now, that is the real reason why so many will not relinquish control of their lives to God. But oh, what they are missing out on! Jesus Christ Himself said, "I am the way the truth and the life. No one comes to the Father but by me." We will live with the results of our decision, and our answer to Christ whether it be yes or no. You cannot reject Jesus Christ and then knock on the door of heaven, demanding or expecting to be let in to God's house and His kingdom. Jesus will meet us there and remind us, "I knocked on your door and you said 'Go away.'"

Just like this book declares in its title, *I Have Seen Too Much!* I can never turn back now. I have experienced the real joy of having fellowship with Christ and can never go back. The joy

I have isn't based on my circumstances or what happens to me. Happiness is so often based on *happenings*. I speak of *joy* and the difference is my perspective of where I stand in my relationship with Jesus, not where I stand in comparison to others.

First, take the time to turn your life over to Jesus. After all, He is the only way you are ever getting off this earth alive. The basics are simple, you have to admit you are a sinner and you can't earn your way to heaven. Then acknowledge Jesus died on the cross for your sins and profess you believe He was raised from the dead and accept the free gift of salvation and invite Jesus into your heart. It is really as simple as it sounds. Do this for your family, do it for yourself, and do it for Jesus who just wants to fill the God-shaped void in your life.

When I say Jesus died for your sins, I mean just that. He died for every sin you ever committed and ever will commit. Don't let your feelings of shame or guilt keep you from this incredible gift. God doesn't serve up shame to His children but offers the 'Bread of Life.' Just like you can't possibly do anything to earn your way into heaven, once you have accepted Jesus into your life, you can't do anything get out of heaven. That's what is known as, 'The Good News,' which is what the word *Gospel* means. One of the hard lessons I have learned is that the pursuit of happiness shouldn't be a pursuit at all. Like the Psalmist says in *Psalm 46:10* *"Be still, and know that I am God" (NKJV)*, if we don't learn to wait on God, then we run the risk of getting ahead of our blessings and never see them for what they are. We ask the question, "Where is God when I need Him?" In reality, He is simply waiting for us to slow down enough to smell the roses again. Remember what that used to be like? We enjoyed the simple pleasures so much before we started the often empty and selfish 'pursuit of happiness.' It was more like chasing the hell out of it. But did we catch it? No, of course not! It was always just out our reach, and the hurrier we went the behinder we got. So, we continue to learn the hard way. We must learn to wait on God.

> *Yet those who wait for the Lord*
> *Will gain new strength;*
> *They will mount up with wings like eagles,*
> *They will run and not get tired,*
> *They will walk and not become weary.* **(Isa. 40:31)**

Step out of the rat race and slow down and smell the roses. Give your wife and kids a great big hug and tell them how much you love them. It is time to get right with God today! So, take a deep breath and look around you; miracles are everywhere if you just take the time to notice them. Make up your mind that when you get up in the morning, you are going to start the day off with your daily dose of *Vitamin 'M.'*

CHOICES

Now that you have read about all these miracles, you now have a choice to make. You can believe they are real, or you can believe that they not; it's your choice. Can they be explained away by some natural explanation, such as coincidence or reexamination of the facts? Are you one of those 'doubting Thomas's' that have to have proof of everything before you believe it? Or are you like the Pharisees in Jesus's time, who refused to believe in miracles because of the implications of what they meant?

You may think that your 'belief' in something requires a scientific explanation. However, "Science doesn't say anything but scientists do," in the words of Frank Turek in his book, *I Don't have Enough Faith to Be an Atheist*. Modern, so-called scientists have an agenda that is so rigid, they will sell their very souls to promote it regardless of where the facts lead. They develop their conclusions first, then bend the facts and warp the truth to match their conclusions, theories, and hypotheses. Intentionally deceptive, they have no moral compass to keep them on the path of truth; in fact, they don't even believe truth exists. Without the burden of truth looming over them, they are 'free' to say anything they want, no matter how absurd.

The word *belief* is an immaterial thing. It cannot be measured or tested or even proven to exist by any scientific means. Likewise, as John Lennox stated in an interview with Eric Metaxas, you cannot prove your wife loves you or that God loves you for that matter (paraphrased). The proof is in the relationships you experience. I have a personal relationship with Jesus; therefore, I know He is real.

Science wants physical proof to believe. I've often heard it said, "I won't believe it unless I can touch it, taste it, feel it, smell it, or see it." We don't really believe that do we? You cannot see love, happiness, joy, reason, imagination, logic, hatred, envy, jealousy, and so forth, but we all know these things to exist and have a tremendous impact on our lives. You cannot see emotions just like you cannot see the wind. But we can see the results of our emotions and the results of the wind blowing. The Canadian college professor, Dr. Jordan Peterson, who was fired for not going along with the 'woke' agenda at his job, stated the truth about science so eloquently, "The universe is NOT made of matter, it is made of WHAT matters." Look around you and see the hatred, violence, crime, and the murder of millions of people often by their own government when so-called 'science' claims life has no meaning, that nothing matters.

Back to your choices. Do you choose to believe in miracles that only happen to you personally? Or does your worldview allow you to even believe in supernatural events at all? If it doesn't, the entire Bible itself must seem to be just myths, legends, and fairy tales. The extraordinary thing is that science itself has discovered irrefutable evidence over the past fifty some odd years about the historical accuracy of the Bible.

Even though scientists have set out to prove that God does not exist as in the 1966 *Time Magazine* cover story declared, "God is Dead." The evidence, according to Eric Metaxas's new book, *Is Atheism Dead?* which is a direct rebuttal to the *Time Magazine* article, has led in the opposite direction and has pointed directly to the existence of a creator. He states even Einstein fudged his numbers in order to lead us away from the fact that the universe had a beginning. When confronted with this, Einstein was forced to retract his conclusions with the statement, "It was the biggest blunder of my life."

My favorite rebuttal to the evolution argument is what evolved first? Your mouth or your butt? Did man starve for a million years or was he constipated for a million years? This is, of course, the argument of irreducible complexity. We have respiratory, circulatory, digestive, nervous, reproductive, vision, olfactory, smell, touch, muscle, skeletal, etc. systems none of which are functional alone or in part. The theory of evolution is so absurdly ridiculous just based on the statistical odds of millions of fortuitous mutations happening by accident. For instance, it is established that the simplest single-celled organism has about 200 component parts and the odds of 200 favorable mutations occurring is about 1 in 10 followed by 60 zeroes. Also, since mutations cannot occur until all 200 functional components are in place the odds are actually zero for any mutations occurring favorable or deleterious. Now imagine, if you will, playing Russian roulette with a revolver with trillions of barrels with only one empty chamber. How many evolutionary scientists would put the gun to their head and pull the trigger hoping to get the empty chamber? Yet I am supposed to believe we are an accident trillions of times more complex than a microorganism? Show me one case, just one case where mutations and natural selection has produced one favorable mutation. When I studied genetics in college 99% of mutations were considered to be fatal to the organism, so with 198 failures out 200 mutations you can see Darwin flunked math as well as all the modern scientists who put their ill-conceived *faith* in evolution. Mutations only destroy existing information not create anything new. It would be like mixing a white cake mix billions of times hoping to produce a chocolate cake. The ingredients are simply not there. The chances of getting a functional DNA strand by accident is in the neighborhood of 1 chance out of 10 with 93,000 zeroes! Even single-celled organisms have DNA like every other living thing on earth including plants. Okay, I know I'm straying a little from the topic at hand, but you get my point. It is time to remove evolution education from our schools and universities. I am not saying replace it with the biblical account of creation. I am just saying its time to take out the trash. If scientists claim it is just a matter of time that a materialistic natural explanation is forthcoming for the origin of life then is time to put up or shut up.

I am not here to debate the merits of science but the merits of the miracles I have witnessed. Can I unequivocally prove they happened? Of course not! Then again, no one else can. That, my friend, is the definition of a miracle. The fact of the matter is that supernatural occurrences are unnatural for man but natural for God. Miracles simply defy human explanation. So, what do you do when you witness a miracle? Do the choices you make in your everyday life change? I would wager that they have to. No one can remain the same after experiencing a miracle first hand. I was forced to change my perspective on just about everything.

The first visible change came in my prayer life. My faith that God was answering my prayers just skyrocketed. The natural outcome of having prayers answered is that you pray more, pray with greater confidence, and have a real expectation that God is listening.

My hunger for biblical truth also became insatiable as I mentioned earlier in the list of authors my daughter encouraged me to read and of course from reading my Bible. I have resorted to downloading podcasts to listen to, especially while I am driving, especially any long distance. *YouTube* has become a valuable tool in finding good biblical scholarship. However, with the current hostility towards all things Christian, I wonder just how long is that going to last? Christian venues are constantly being removed from YouTube. Censorship is already rampant and out of control as you all know only too well. Social media platforms, like so many of our institutions, have been taken over by left-leaning progressives bent on censoring the truth and silencing the Christian voice. It is to the peril of our freedom, our well-being, our safety and security, and the survival of our very civilization, culture, and country.

It is time to make your choice. You will either choose to go along to get along, or you will choose to take a stand. If we choose not to believe in miracles, then the greatest miracle of all, the resurrection, will mean nothing to you. What is the real result of my witnessing such a broad array of miracles? Isaiah says it best:

> *Now, therefore, fear the Lord and serve Him in sincerity and truth; and put away the gods which your fathers served beyond the River and in Egypt, and serve the Lord. If it is disagreeable in your sight to serve the Lord,* **choose for yourselves today whom you will serve:** *whether the gods which your fathers served which were beyond the River, or the gods of the Amorites in whose land you are living;* **but as for me and my house, we will serve the Lord. (Isa. 24:14–15)**

Author's Bio:

Terry Capehart is a City Planner with a Master's Degree in City and Regional Planning from the University of Texas at Arlington. He retired in 2016 after a distinguished career of public service in eight different North Texas communities. His 'Great Cloud of Witnesses' are long-time friends and colleagues who so graciously shared their stories as well as provided comfort and prayer support over the decades without which I couldn't have developed such an unshakable faith.

Terry Capehart
Royse City, Texas

tlcplanning@zoho.com

CPSIA information can be obtained
at www.ICGtesting.com
Printed in the USA
LVHW080427201222
735289LV00017B/2992